A Life Half Told

Unraveling my story through DNA

William Aperance & Courtney Aperance

Cover Design by Elizabeth Mackey

Paperback ISBN: 9798876674975

To my wife and children, who encouraged and supported me through this journey.

To my siblings, step and half, who I have shared some, part, and all of my life with.

Contents

Prologue

I did not plan to write a memoir. I do not believe that people are urged to write about their life until something changes its trajectory, or forces them to reevaluate all they once knew, making sense of what they lived.

I never thought my story would be interesting enough to share. My traumatic childhood memories and experiences, tucked away in my brain like an old dusty box in the attic, never felt like a narrative that deserved to be retold. I certainly didn't want to relive them.

But then it happened. A playful curiosity brought a discovery that would forever change my life. So, what could I do? Presented with the opportunity to open locked boxes, some long before I knew they existed. After all, were these boxes meant for me to uncover? Were these stories meant to be retold? Finally, I was given a key. A key that would unlock my past and explain my present. A key to every box hidden in the attic.

I have written this memoir to share an amazing story about a stranger who came unexpectedly into my life, forcing me to reexamine everything about myself, my life's journey, and what I knew to be true.

Christmas

"So, get a load of this one!" my eldest son Billy said to my wife over the phone. "It looks like my DNA results say I'm twenty-five percent Italian!" My wife, Kim, said later that she found it amusing, not alarming in any way, even though it was unexpected. It was just one of the many "who woulda thunk it" moments we often shared at dinner or over the phone. Both my wife and I and our kids had worked with the public for years. Imponderables were our meat and potatoes.

"Hey, honey...did you hear that?" Kim yelled in my direction, through two rooms to the family room where I was ensconced in my after-hours recliner. "Billy's DNA results say he's a quarter Italian. Did somebody jump over the fence on your side of the family that we don't know about?" She gave up talking across the house and returned to our son. "If this is true, your father better learn how to make sauce and meatballs on Sunday," she said, and her lovely laugh bounced off the kitchen walls, warming the whole house.

I was taking my usual weekend retreat in front of the fireplace, allowing my cigar smoke to drift up the chimney and away into the manicured forest surrounding our home in upstate New York.

I often watched mindless TV to unwind, with my dog Sadie sleeping by my side. That day it was *Two and a Half Men*. Not that it mattered. It was just white noise to distract me from the cares of the week. I could hear Kim putzing around the kitchen, cleaning up dinner, and talking to our son on speaker—the comforting sounds of home.

Kim and Billy spoke almost every day. Billy was in his midthirties and moved out west to Nevada upon graduating college, but he and his mother had remained as close as they had always been. I spoke to him less frequently, but I kept up with him through his mother. And now, he had gone and turned Italian on me without even discussing the matter, and apparently, I was now signed up to make meatballs and Sunday gravy!

I wasn't surprised when Billy decided to do one of those DNA kits. He had always been curious about anything scientific, and we encouraged him to follow what interested him. Kim was so excellent, seeing Billy for who he was and embracing that. It took me a little longer to accept that my son wasn't interested in Pop Warner football, Little League, or soccer. While most kids spent their summers playing kickball, swimming in their pools, and riding their bikes around the neighborhood, Billy asked to attend science camps for engineering and genetics. So we found physics and robotics programs through his school. He flourished, and made many friends who shared similar interests.

Since he was a kid, Billy had asked Kim and me endless questions about our family history. He seemed to enjoy making sense of his heritage. We told him everything we knew, which honestly wasn't much. In hindsight, not many of the stories we told him were accurate; they were more like legends passed down year after year. An oral tradition that changed a little each time the tale was told. Kind of like an intergenerational game of telephone.

Years earlier, my cousin, Denis, had embarked upon an extensive research project into our family tree, and we got a real sense of where we came from. Denis did it old school, with charts and diagrams all drawn out on graph paper. None of us questioned his results. Denis told us that he had traced our lineage to four Lithuanian brothers who lived in the New York Tri-State area in the first half of the last century. So, when my son came up with so much Italy in his veins, I assumed the Lithuanians might have also been part Italian.

It didn't seem like a big deal. We all knew what went on at Ellis Island in those days and how often mistakes were made. We figured somebody checked the wrong box in the early 1900s, and we laughed about it. It never even occurred to me that since my wife had zero Italian in her DNA, my quarter-Italian son would have to come from a half-Italian father. Sometime in the next few months, Kim took her DNA, and Billy started a family tree. Her results were predictable. Her ancestors came from England, Scandinavia, and Germany, which matched what we knew.

I didn't think about my genetic past again until Christmas morning the following year. All the kids were home for the holiday, and although it was almost noon, they were still asleep.

"Some things never change!" my wife said with a chuckle. "It's eleven a.m. on Christmas morning, and we must wake the kids up." We'd been waking them up to open presents on Christmas morning for over thirty years. Our whole family was on restaurant time. We stayed up late and loved to sleep in, even on Christmas morning. This was all our fault, of course. Kim and I began a Christmas Eve tradition when the kids were toddlers. We would serve platters of finger foods for us and snacks for the kids, and we'd stay up late, playing board games, laughing, and enjoying this special time together. After our years working in some of the finest country clubs, the snacks became more extensive and turned into a charcuterie board of fine cheeses, pâtés, French baguettes, smoked mussels, oysters, and salami. We spent every Christmas Eve feasting on what we called "our tray" full of delicacies.

This year, one by one, the kids came downstairs and found their usual place on the couch or the overstuffed leather chair. Everyone knew Dad had dibs on the recliner. Our artificial tree was now twenty years old but still had a great shape, and the branches remained full. We decorated it with our usual gold and red ribbons, bows and balls, and, most significantly, our cherished family ornaments. Our family legacy dangled on those branches: stars with our children's kindergarten smiles, hand-painted snowmen, every family dog we've loved, and destinations where we vacationed together. The tree was prettier and more meaningful every year.

"Who wants coffee?" Kim asked once everybody had managed to make their way downstairs. She was wearing the new pajamas I had given her the night before, following our traditional Christmas gift tradition. Bradley, our middle son, claimed his space on the couch. Bradley was tall like his brother, topping six feet two inches and just as bright. However, his interest was in business management, and he quickly changed his major to accounting after arriving at State University of New York at Geneseo. Like his brother, he got an excellent job out of college and began his career auditing with a local accounting firm. Like his parents, he turned out to be a workaholic, and quickly became the youngest VP in his company. We've always been so very proud of him.

With James Taylor Christmas songs playing softly in the background, my daughter Courtney grew impatient to open the presents. Even now in her thirties, she still loved the magic of Christmas. She was different from her older brothers, although just as intelligent and extremely funny. Blonde and beautiful like her mother, she didn't grow as tall as the boys. She has described herself perfectly on her Instagram account: "Teacher by day, wedding crasher by night, sangria drinking, puppy snuggling, sunshine loving life enthusiast!".

Kim distributed the colorful packages from under the tree. We opened one at a time so that everyone could enjoy each gift together. Kim was an experienced and meticulous Santa. She always knew which gifts went to who and in what order, and everyone got most of what they asked for. I would take my usual spot in my recliner, watching as everyone opened their gifts one by one, groaning whenever they passed another gift my way. With every gift I received, I had a sense of unworthiness. Even though most of the time, it was your average Christmas essentials, socks, ties, and the occasional phone case, I always felt uncomfortable and wished they hadn't spent their hard-earned money on me.

Once all the gifts were opened, I went to the kitchen to make Christmas brunch. I was always the chef for this much-anticipated meal. "Wait! Here's one more for you, Daddy," Kim called to me, handing me a small, poorly wrapped box from behind the tree. I could always pick out Courtney's presents based on the lousy wrap job. I tore it open excitedly and saw "Ancestry" written on the front of the box. I looked at her quizzically. Why had she given me a DNA test for Christmas?

"C'MON! Billy took one, Mom took one, and I even did the doggie one on Tucker!" Courtney said, her big, brown eyes sparkling, with her smile lighting up the room. "Now it's your turn!"

"It would be interesting to see yours, Dad," Billy chimed in. "You never know what could show up."

"Thank you, sweetie," I said, and hugged my daughter. I laid the kit next to my pile of loot under the tree and went off to make brunch. Our traditional family Christmas brunch menu was sausage, bacon, hash browns, and eggs—any style. We served up the eggnog and mimosas.

"How do you want your eggs?" I shouted, without even turning from the skillet. It was scrambled for everyone except Billy and me, with our usual choice of eggs poached on English muffins. Eric, who I've worked with for over twenty years in three different clubs, always gave us a loaf of his homemade pumpkin bread, a dessert in and of itself. I never had to announce "breakfast is ready." I raised a family of eaters with good sniffers, so they readily followed the smell and gathered around the table just as I was pulling the cinnamon buns out of the oven.

This was our favorite time of the year, and the only holiday when we could all be together, just the five of us. In our role as a management team at a private country club, Kim and I have always worked through all the other holidays: Easter, Mother's Day, Thanksgiving, Memorial and Labor Day, Fourth of July, and New Year's Eve. Private country clubs would be exceptionally busy on holidays, and it was up to Kim and me to ensure everything went smoothly. When the kids were little, Kim and I worked many nights and weekends and relied heavily on babysitters and family members to care for the kids. In the summer, we could send them to a camp just down the road from the club so that I could drop them off on my way to work. Then, depending on our schedules, Kim or I would alternate leaving work earlier and taking them home. As the kids got older, we were fortunate enough that our positions allowed us to provide them with jobs. This helped them all learn to be responsible, hardworking, and independent, and they learned to manage their own money at a young age. But, ironically, the most important benefit for us was seeing our kids at work and spending more time together.

Courtney, our youngest and only daughter, gravitated towards the club business more than our boys did, especially when it came to activities for the kids. By the time she was twelve years old, she was babysitting for the members' kids during our "Parents' Night Out." Eventually, she became my camp director. Courtney was always interested in working with children, so we weren't surprised when she achieved her dream of becoming an elementary school teacher. From the age of fifteen, she maintained a part-time server job at the club, working two jobs to make extra money to pay off her student loans.

***

Looking around the table as we finished enjoying our brunch, a feeling of gratitude came over me. We were all together for a well-deserved holiday. Kim and I have always been proud that we were able to raise such responsible and hardworking kids.

My family always starts to coordinate the annual Aperance Christmas gathering a few months in advance. It rotates to different homes yearly, often landing on a date after the holiday. This was our year. Kim was also strategic with how and when she would remind me of this.

"Don't forget, it's our turn to do the Aperance party..." Kim said cautiously, waiting for my reaction.

"Are you sure? It seems like it's here every year!" I replied, as my neck tightened. The truth is, I knew it was our year, and I had already begun preparing myself for it. I missed many family gatherings for decades, primarily because our work schedules required Kim and me to work weekends in the summer months. We would miss several picnics and backyard parties, but I always made it to the Christmas one.

These family gatherings made me uneasy. Just like the feeling I got that one time driving the Pacific Coast Highway from Napa to

San Francisco, when I had to turn around and take the alternate route, or the way my stomach sinks any time I am higher than three feet off the ground. Don't get me wrong; I loved my family and liked seeing them. However, being with them often brought back memories. They were all lovely people who I adored. Unfortunately, they just happened to be reminders of the life I spent years trying to avoid.

The House that Jeffers Built

My mother, Ann, was raised as an only child, adopted by her great-aunt and uncle, Catherine and Lewis Jeffers. Lewis was a well-known and respected architect and homebuilder in the area who was responsible for numerous high-end residential neighborhoods in nearby Glenville, New York. He even had one of the streets named "Catherine" after his beloved wife.

The Jeffers were local Dutch Reformed Church members and were well-off for the times and the area. As a builder, he purchased a large parcel of land from Catherine's sister Mary Larrabee and her husband Emerson, a few miles west of Scotia, NY, on a two-lane highway west of Amsterdam. And, of course, the largest, most expensive house he ever built was his own.

Emerson and Mary had three daughters, Lois, Ginny, and Althea, and a son, Raymond. Their daughter, Althea, suffered significant mental health issues and could not care for her daughter, my mother. The Jefferses were older and quite wealthy when they took in my mother and in and adopted her. So naturally, she was spoiled her whole life. She was given the world, complete with her own pony and a large-scale stand-up playhouse replicating the big house she lived in, with pillars, doors, and windows.

For the late fifties, this was a stunning property by any measure, and rightly worth a small fortune. The main house was opulent for the era. It would have been considered a McMansion of the time: custom mahogany woodworking, solid oak flooring throughout, and filled with the best furnishings, fixtures, and modern appliances you could buy at the time. As an architect and homebuilder, Lewis could build himself and Catherine the finest home in the area. He was contracted to build another family the same house a few miles closer to the village of Scotia, which he did, but smaller.

My grandparents' house was a gray stucco with ivy climbing the exterior walls and reaching for the sunlight. Lilacs and rhododendrons surrounded a white trim, full-length sunroom. A driveway came in on the left side of the house but circled the entire structure. Jeffers designed a large front yard, although smaller than the Larrabees' next door, but large enough for us to play baseball as kids. In front, large white pillars held up the roof over a huge front porch. A grand entrance led to a vast staircase that went straight up to a large landing and several steps more, returning to the second floor. Off the main foyer, leading into the dining room and living room, were gorgeous wooden oak pocket doors that disappeared into the walls when opened. On the right was a huge dining room with a crystal chandelier, a massive built-in china cabinet the length of the far wall, with a center mirror. Straight ahead under the stairway landing was the most exquisite grandfather clock, standing a good eight feet tall. I would stare at the pendulum and the weights rising and falling, waiting for the clock to chime the correct number of times. On the right of the staircases was a large front hall walk-in closet with dozens of coats and hats, including the most luxurious mink fur coats, and fox and raccoon wraps with the heads still intact. Every time I would go into the closet their black beady eyes stared out as the smell of mothballs surrounded me, filling the foyer.

Upstairs were four huge bedrooms, tiled bathroom floors, and two porcelain bathtubs, one larger than the other, with decorative lion's feet. The upstairs foyer was a huge linen closet that covered the entire far wall from floor to ceiling, holding spare sheets, pillows, and blankets.

The kitchen had all the modern appliances, including a steel stove with ceramic doors, classic for that period. The living room was exquisite, the length of the house with a beautiful fireplace. The chimney breast also went up to another fireplace in the main bedroom. Handmade cabinets with doors made of lead and glass flanked the fireplace, full of books, games left from when my mother was a child, and essential papers. Above the doors was a long mantel with an exquisite clock.

At the back of the main house was a garage with two complete apartments, one upstairs and one on the rear side, still leaving room off the garage for a giant tool shed with every piece of equipment and small tool necessary to maintain the property. The garage was large enough to house what was my mother's prized possession, purchased for her by the Jefferses. It was a 1956 white Cadillac convertible with a red leather interior. You know, the one with the distinctive bullet-shaped boobies in the front bumper. I can't think of that car now without realizing that she treated that car better than any of us children. I do not recall ever riding in it, but would go into the garage just to sit in it. Behind the oversized garage were additional red sheds that once housed Grandpa Jeffers's tool benches, larger mowing equipment, and tractors.

You could tell by the tools he amassed that he had meticulously trimmed and sprayed insecticides on his small orchard. That man obsessively trimmed, pruned, and sprayed pesticides on the beautiful cherry, apple, and pear trees in his backyard, which he tended to religiously. After Grandpa Jeffers passed away, we would climb these trees to get the best fruit. I would sit on a branch eating cherries, spitting out the pits until my stomach hurt. Throughout the large yard were very elegant concrete birdbaths, stone benches, a sundial, perennial flowering bushes, grapes on a white lattice arbor, and trees strategically planted decades earlier and thriving. Raspberries and blackberries grew wild along the fences, and a few vegetable patches had crops that could be preserved. Oh man, the rhubarb. We used to just eat the crimson-red stalks right out of the garden. We could smell the fruit trees and flower garden everywhere. From the garage, you entered a traditional root cellar, which stored dozens of Ball jars all filled with Grandma Jeffers's preserved jellies, jams, jarred peaches, pears, and applesauce. In addition to the fruit trees, Lewis was an avid beekeeper and cared for many chickens and hens. I guess we were vegetarians, mostly eating fruits and vegetables all summer and then cherries, apples, and pears into the fall.

I vaguely remember images of Grandpa Jeffers, as I was pretty young when he passed. I'm not sure I ever remember talking to him or bouncing on his knee. Their yard was a perfect playground for a young child. However, by the time we were old enough to wander around on our own, it was evident that he could no longer care for the property like he used to, with remnants of feathers in the remaining chicken coops. He no longer tended to the beehives, which were all still there, but now they would chase or swarm any of us if we got too close. As a result, we got stung weekly. I was very allergic, and many times my face would blow up until I couldn't open my eyes. He stopped spraying the bees, but they thrived for years after, with the flower gardens and devouring the fruit that lay on the ground.

I remember my father was around helping him mow for a few years, doing what he could until Grandpa Jeffers passed. The Jefferses loved my father, especially since he was not Italian, like my mother's first husband whom they despised. However, there was no one to keep up with the pruning and pesticide applications that kept the apple and cherry trees blooming and providing an abundance of beautiful fruit. The blackberries, strawberries, and rhubarb patches became overgrown, and no one was left to maintain them. The cellar remained cool, and dust and cobwebs covered the jars. The well-manicured farm that once bloomed became a run-down shadow of its past.

The Larrabees, my mother's biological family, were "salt of the earth" people. On their large farm, their house was set quite a way back off the road. Behind their house was an elongated garage with several doors where they were always working on cars, trucks, and tractors. Their property also extended down to the river and probably was three or four times the size of the Jeffers property next door, but their property widened as it went back. Both properties were large, with hundreds of acres of land each, running down to the Mohawk River.

The Larrabees' house was a much older, wooden house with an addition from the fifties which gave them their first indoor bathroom. I distinctly remember this bathroom as it looked out of a movie, large and lavish with black and white linoleum square tiles in a checkerboard design and a similar elegant bathtub to the Jeffers.

An upright piano and an open-hearth fireplace prominently displaying a WWII helmet were in their living room. The helmet belonged to my Uncle Raymond. Since I was my father's firstborn male, he wanted me to take his name, William. My middle name was a tribute to my mother's uncle, who was killed in the war. Everyone called me Billy except my Aunt Lois and the Larrabee side of the family. They called me Billy Ray. It was really enjoyable becoming the standing joke in middle school when everyone realized my initials spelled BRA.

Behind the garage and throughout the middle of their property were broken-down, rusted cars, trucks, and tractors abandoned and kept for parts, but it was like a theme park for a six-year-old boy who wanted to play in every one of them. Each had a distinct smell of musty moisture that deteriorated seats and permeated every remaining fabric piece. Some were stripped, and we would sit on the open seat springs and pretend to shift the cars.

In my later years living next door in the Jefferses' home, I remember Grandpa Larrabee sitting on his front porch in a metal chair that rocked from early morning until the end of the day. He sat there with a pad and pencil enjoying his life, as he was probably in his late eighties, counting dump trucks coming and going into the back of his property. He had turned his hundreds of acres into a very profitable stone quarry and would count the trucks leaving filled with rock and stone, figuring how much money he made that day. We all loved going next door to visit the Larrabees. Aunt Mary Larrabee would have cruller donuts and would tell us kids amusing stories of when she was a child, like the one about how her mom would bake pies and set them on the kitchen window to cool. She said that the Mohawk Native Americans would come and steal them, so they would make extra to have enough for everyone. I recently learned another version of this story, that they were most likely drifters that would be traveling by way of railroad cars looking for food.

My Parents

Somewhere between the time my mother was a spoiled child enjoying her playhouse and the feisty age of sixteen, she grew into what must have been an ungrateful, self-centered teenager. This wild, rebellious side of her, I'm sure, is what led her to become pregnant with her first daughter Toni, forcing her into a marriage with Ernest Conti that lasted just long enough for her son Ernest (known to the family as Butch), the second of her burdensome children, to be born.

Catherine and Lewis tried to maintain control of her irrational behavior. Against the Jefferses' strict orders, my mother had also begun a relationship with her biological father, Walt Rice, which infuriated her adoptive parents. They gave her a choice; live with them under their rules or go with her father, who abandoned her as a child. Without hesitation, she left for a short time with her two children to live with her biological father.

Grandpa Rice owned a small business capitalizing on the new jukebox craze of the fifties, providing jukeboxes and, eventually, pinball machines to bars and restaurants throughout the area. He would then go around collecting all the quarters in the locked drawer, giving the proprietor a small cut of the take. This was normal, since he had to purchase the costly machines, keep an inventory of thousands of records, and maintain them whenever drunks slammed into them or just with the usual expected wear and tear. They were extremely popular, and Grandpa Rice made a very nice living.

However, Ann quickly realized it made more sense for her to return to her adopted parents at the "big house" and move into the garage apartment to help them around the property, most likely due to her nearing an inheritance.

My mother's feisty personality, mixed with her bombshell looks, I'm sure, made her sought after by any James Dean wannabe wearing denim jeans and a white tee shirt with a cigarette pack rolled up in his sleeve. My father fit this description to a T. I'm not sure she ever shared when and why the first marriage failed, but it wasn't too long after that divorce or even before that my mother met my father, Bill. He was a handsome man who would frequent the same bars, playing the drums in local trios or bands—an easy target for my mother. Sadly, Butch and Toni were not the last of her unexpected and unwanted pregnancies. My father fell in love, and with two toddlers, and before the ink was dry on her first divorce, my mother became pregnant with my older sister Laurie. No one knows whether she left Ernest Conti before my father was in the picture or quickly after, but there she was, pregnant with my father's first child, and now a mother of three before her twenty-first birthday.

My parents eventually married in '53, quickly followed by my birth in October of '54 and my sister Debbie only eleven months later, in September of '55. As they settled into their new life, Grandpa Jeffers, the Larrabees, and my father built a four-room wooden house on a concrete slab where the chicken coops once stood. We lived in that flat-roofed, elongated house, similar to a fabricated house today, for a few years when I was a toddler.

Two years later, they had my youngest sister Rae Ann, followed by my brother, Jeffery, in 1960.

Gram

When my parents got married, and Laurie was born, my father moved his mother into a small apartment in the back of the garage. Grandma Mary, or "Gram" as she was affectionately called, was a lovely lady of German descent who grew up in NYC on the East Side. She married William Joseph Aperance, a small "off-Broadway" theater manager. When my father was about ten years old, his father left town, or as my grandmother always told us, "He went out for a pack of smokes and never came back." But as I have learned, there are two sides to every story, and my grandmother, as pleasant as she was, was also pretty tough, and probably kicked his ass out for some valid reason.

My father never spoke of my grandfather. They lived in Brooklyn, and my father spent most of his free time playing baseball in the sand lots around Ebbet's Field. I knew he always harbored a deep resentment for being abandoned by his father, even if my grandmother shared some of the blame. My father was quite athletic, and after years of crushing balls in those old sand lots, he ultimately earned a place on the Brooklyn Dodgers farm team. Gram would show everyone who came to her house the picture of him poised at first base in his minor league uniform. "Here is your father playing first base for the Brooklyn Dodgers!" she would proudly point out. He would share stories about his time in Brooklyn, and spoke of friends he grew up with who also found their way up north to the Capital Region around Albany. My father was a hard worker, in and out of welding and construction, where it was always a struggle for him to find year-long work. My mother never worked while I was growing up, having seven kids to manage.

Gram was one of our relatives who always had a steady job. She spent years working at this same upscale furniture store as the office manager. They had five locations in other nearby towns, and they moved a lot of furniture, as it was high quality and just the right price point for most of the young General Electric engineers employed at the company's large Schenectady headquarters. So, she began purchasing her furniture from their store with some good discounts. I remember her house was immaculate with the best furniture. Luckily, Gram also purchased our family's first Brownie camera, maybe the only camera for many years. She took all our childhood pictures and lined us up by age and height in every picture, whether outside or sitting on the couch. Especially at Easter, she ensured we were all dressed in the new clothes she purchased for us. I'm pretty sure we did not attend any Easter services, but we were all dressed in our Sunday best so she could get a picture of us. Although she was not as wealthy as Grandma and Grandpa Jeffers, she was always well-kept, with her frequent visits to her beauty parlor on State Street to get her hair permed. She also was impeccably dressed, owning dozens of shoes that she would dye to match her dresses, and had a splendid complexion she credited to her use of only Ivory soap on her face her whole life.

Gram was our rock in life. She was gentle and intelligent, with a toughness that she showed when necessary. When we had a cold, each of us would find our way to Gram's apartment so she could take care of us. Regardless of the illness, she would rub Vicks on our chest and stick a few globs up our nostrils. She was there for all our bouts with chicken pox and measles and anytime we needed to hide from the fighting and chaos. Having her live on the same property during these tumultuous years growing up was a godsend. In hindsight, I don't know if our lives would have been the same without her. Laurie was my father's firstborn, so when my parents split up or had knockdown dragged-out fights, she usually stayed with Gram, while we younger children were sent off with various other relatives. Gram tried to remain neutral between my parents, knowing that her son had numerous flaws and my mother had just as many, if not more. She protected us from harm as best she could and tried to do whatever she could to preserve the family unit. The thought of what would have happened to us children during those ten years they were together if my grandmother was not there for us makes me shudder.

Growing up at the Big House

In her early twenties, my mother was a stunningly beautiful woman, resembling Lucille Ball. Yet she was incapable of ever feeling satisfied, resulting in her seven children, two by her first husband. Did she believe the more children she had increased her life satisfaction? Or were we all just the result of her impulsive, attention-seeking behavior, craving even the smallest amount of devotion from a man? She joked when I was a toddler and she was pregnant with Rae Ann, and said, "All your father had to do was to hang his pants on the bedpost, and I was pregnant again." She named each daughter with Ann as their middle name. Toni Ann, Laurie Ann, Debbie Ann, and Rae Ann. This may have seemed cute then, but it was probably just another sign of her narcissism and excessive need for admiration. Plus, she named my brother Jeff-ERY, not the traditional spelling of every other Jeff-REY born. She filled out the form incorrectly in the hospital and was most likely incapable of admitting she made a mistake; she stuck by it. She purposely spelled it that way because there was no way it could have been wrong.

When Grandpa Jeffers passed away, my mother took advantage of her father's death, relocating her mother into the small apartment above the garage so she, my father, and all five of us kids could move out of the wooden structure on the slab and into the Big House. That house had four bedrooms, each room large enough for two four-poster beds with carved spindles. The girls shared two bedrooms, and Butch had his own until I was old enough to sleep with him. Before then, my bed (or crib turned into a bed) was in the closet off my mother's bathroom, which was a large walk-in with a window overlooking the front porch roof. That is where I slept as a toddler, and, in hindsight, with the proximity to her bedroom, my sweet, innocent eyes probably saw much too much.

I remember watching her gaze into a full-length mahogany mirror as she dressed to go out for the evening. The main bedroom, which used to belong to her parents, was large and opulent, complete with a fireplace, a large four-poster bed, and the most gorgeous mahogany dressers. I would peek through the cracked door to watch as she admired herself. The old keyholes back then were quite large, and a small eye could see much of the room without any trouble. She extended the end of her lipstick, the bright red color gliding across her pursed lips.

She was headed out to dinner at the restaurant down the street, which my parents frequented regularly. They often dressed up and headed out for the evening, always returning intoxicated and ready to attack, like feral cats and dogs. It was the same "song and dance" each time. As a tough guy, my father was a mean drunk and would exacerbate the entire incident with his drunken temper. My mother was only able to infuriate him more with her anger issues, and just as violent. The fights sometimes had to be broken up by Gram, unless it got so bad she or my mother would call the police. One time, I remember seeing her holding back one of her large German shepherds. "I'll let my dogs loose on you!" she threatened as the dog growled and snarled, pulling on the chain-link choke collar. "Go ahead!" my father stammered. "I'll wrap that dog around your neck, and you'll have one less dog to feed!" We all knew what was likely to happen, so when they returned, we would wait to hear the fighting start. Then we would sneak quietly out of bed, crawl down to the landing, and peek through the spindles of the enormous staircase overlooking the large foyer to hear and see them scream and fight, sometimes leading to physical abuse. And Gram would be there each time and try to break them up. The local police were called numerous times, which always ended in the same way, with them hauling my father away for the night to sleep it off. One time, I specifically remember he physically fought with the arresting officers. He might have been incarcerated for a night or possibly longer, depending on whether my mother filed charges. More often than not, all charges were dropped by morning once everyone sobered up.

The memories I have of my childhood are minimal, as any positive moments are buried, overshadowed by the tough times that vividly remain. I have to assume that we had some happy family times, but very few come to mind. A faint recollection of somewhat peaceful times was sitting around our new color TV to watch *The Wizard of Oz*, *Walt Disney's Wonderful World of Color*, and the historic moment when The Beatles appeared on *The Ed Sullivan Show*.

As a young toddler living in the small prefab house I remember the excitement we all felt about going to the big house. Grandma Jeffers would make a big family dinner on Sundays. We got to eat in the big dining room with a large chandelier and custom mahogany china closets along the far wall, under a huge center mirror. It was magnificent, and I looked forward to these Sunday visits. We would surround the elongated table, and all sit in the oversized formal chairs, dazzled by the shiny silverware and freshly pressed lace doily napkins. After dinner, we would play in the living room on the carpet with classic toys still left from when my mother was a child: Chinese checkers, pick-up sticks, and a real wind-up jack-in-the-box that would pop up and scare everyone into a fit of laughter. We all knew that we had to be on our best behavior, or we would get a spanking when we went home. No one ever misbehaved.

I remember piling into the station wagon with our cousins to go to the drive-in theater. These were "the good ol' days," when you paid the entry fee per car, not per person, so we all had to squeeze to save money. One night, in the middle of summer, *The Birds* by Alfred Hitchcock was playing on the screen, and I distinctly remember the nauseous pit I had in my stomach after eating way too much candy and swinging way too high on the swings near the concession stand. Rest assured, that was the first and last time I would ever eat black licorice.

Christmases as a child in the big house must have been somewhat joyous, although unmemorable, with minimal gifts of clothes, pajamas, and a few toys purchased mainly by Gram, with my mother not working, and my father usually laid off because of lack of work in the brutal northeastern winter. Amazingly, none of my siblings can remember specific toys or Christmas memories from these first ten years in the big house, a time of chaos, fighting, and lack of individual attention or receiving daily parental love. My parents seemed to be going through the motions and not emphasizing the importance of Christmas, family, and love. There was none of that shit!

Birthdays were no different, and we don't remember much surrounding them. However, my grandmother did see that we were entered to be on the local Freddie Freihofer show. They would invite twenty to thirty kids who were having their birthday that month, televise the kids all dressed up, and give each one a birthday cake. My older siblings had gone on the show, and I was so excited when it was my turn. We all piled in the station wagon and drove over the bridge. As the reality of being on TV sunk in, I started kicking and screaming that I didn't want to do it. I didn't want to be seen or looked at by anyone. By the time we pulled into the WRGB TV station parking lot, I was having a full-blown anxiety attack, and no one could understand why, since I was so excited leading up to that day. I refused to move. They couldn't get me to go in, and we returned home.

Cousins

We had several aunts and uncles who lived very close, so we often spent a lot of time with our cousins. Margaret, my mother's younger sister, had five children with Walter Strait. Their son, Walt Strait, was my age, as was Bobby Rice, the oldest son of my mother's brother Robert. We were always getting into trouble together. We rarely went to their house, even though it was very close. Bobby and his family lived in a two-room house built on the Larrabee property. It seemed as if they always spent time at our house, since it was much larger and there was always something to do. We would spend hours exploring the property and finding ways to get into trouble. We would play behind the Larrabee house, in the fields strewn with old cars, trucks, tractors, and even a hearse. We would jump from one to the other and pretend to drive and shift the cars, even though they all smelled of rust and mildew from what remained of the rotting seats and headliners. It was a playground for any young boy, and tetanus shots were just waiting to happen. We also rode bikes down to the gravel pit, as we referred to it, where the Larrabees sold the excavating rights to a local company that, over several years, took out thousands of dump trucks filled with stone and gravel. By then, it was a large quarry well over a hundred acres and dozens of stories deep.

The Straits lived a mile away from us on a dirt road with several old and shabby homes, none as bad as theirs. Like my mother, my aunt, who was her younger sister, had five children, despite being unable to afford one. Margaret and Walter would spend virtually every night at the little bar that was, unfortunately for my cousins, at the end of their road, where they would spend the bulk of their paychecks every week then crawl home. Even as a youngster, I was acutely aware of the poor conditions and neglect that my cousins endured. They all slept on old filthy mattresses scattered on the floor throughout the small rooms, without sheets and with burlap bags as blankets. There was a smell of urine and the stench of dirty clothes and garbage strewn around. These images are still as clear as yesterday, burnt into my memory like a bad piece of toast. The contrast was stark, and I learned very young that how we and our cousins lived was not the norm. Both Margeret and Walter would, if they weren't already, turn out to be certifiable alcoholics, and their children were eventually removed from their homes by child protective custody; the older children even ended up placed in a state-run facility that decades later was found to have allowed sexual abuse of many children for years without stopping it.

I'm grateful for my ability to recognize how terrible these conditions were at such a young age, and that it left such an impression on me. I credit my time spent with Uncle Bill and Aunt Lois, where I was able to see a stark difference in all our living conditions.

Our families spent a lot of time together before my mother was hospitalized. My father hated the fact that he would often come home from work to find that Aunt Margaret and her ragamuffins were there, which created even more tension between my parents. It got so bad that when my father approached the house after work, he would keep driving if he saw their car and make a beeline to the nearest tavern. Of course, this was probably just an excuse not to come home and to get drunk instead, which always ended badly.

They must have agreed that moving away from the Big House and our cousins might be a way to save the marriage, so they rented a house closer to where my father worked as a welder. But unfortunately, it was also closer to several bars my father would frequent for lunch and after work before heading home to the chaos.

Tower Ave

I still remember Jeffery being brought home from the hospital, my parents proudly walking up to the front of our new house to show him off to us kids and Gram, who had watched us until they returned. Jeffery was my mother's seventh child, the fifth for my father.

It turned out a new house and a new baby were not the answer to their problems. Their relationship did not get any better, and as I recall, my father always seemed drunk, fighting with my mother, who would go on unnecessary tirades. I'm sure having seven kids in a small house, struggling to make ends meet, and coming home to a hostile environment, which was as much as his making as my mother's, who was by this time an emotional basket case, were all triggers.

I recall one night in June; we had just sat down for dinner. It was becoming exceptionally humid and eerie outside as the wind picked up. It was obvious a storm was brewing, but we had no idea to what extent. Just then, the strong winds shook the house, blowing out windows and knocking everything off the shelves. The canned beets we were eating ended up every-where. The winds were so strong they knocked the china cabi-

net over, leaving every glass and dish shattered. It was an F3 tornado with hundred-and-forty-mile-an-hour winds that cut right
through the town of Rotterdam and across our street, putting us
in the eye of the storm. Now, this was not the first time remnants
of smashed dishes lay across the house as though a tornado had
ripped through; it just happened to be the first time my mother
had the weather to blame and not my father.

This was also about the time my mother, without a doubt,
had been suffering from years of postpartum depression, which I
now feel ultimately manifested in severe depression and was the
cause of her anger and resentment towards her children. She could
not emotionally handle the turmoil and the daily interaction that,
understandably, would come from having seven kids at that time,
ranging from two to twelve years of age. Even with her attempt at
strict discipline, we continued to make daily life worse for her, like
when we pulled all the feathers from our pillows and threw them
out the second-floor bedroom window. Oh, what a sight that must
have been. Now that I think about what we dumped on her, maybe
we were just as much to blame as my father's drinking for my
mother's reactive behavior. Ultimately, surprising no one, starting
over in their own new house was not the magical cure they had
hoped for, and things just got worse. Before we knew it, only after
a year or so, we were heading back to the Big House. In hindsight,
the whirlwind that occurred in our house that night was not the
only windstorm that existed for my parents; the F3 tornado and
their marriage were equally turbulent.

Back to the Big House

As we reestablished ourselves in the big house, my mother's mental condition only worsened, and her relationship with my father was more unstable than ever. For many years, she was under doctor's care until finally, in the spring of 1962, in coordination with her local ob-gyn, she voluntarily admitted herself into a state-run mental hospital in Utica, NY, about an hour west of where we lived. She stayed at the New York State psychiatric hospital for several months. I'd like to believe she tried her best to get healthy, yet by the fall, she voluntarily checked herself out and returned home.

It was obvious she wasn't better. Following her return, my parents found it more and more difficult to live with one another, and life became intolerable for all of us. With my mother's irrational behavior, my father's continuous drinking binges, and the pure exhaustion of fighting, they finally separated for good in 1963 and were divorced in 1965.

My mother was now the sole parent, yet not emotionally stable enough to properly raise one child, let alone all seven of us. Until then, my father had shared in doling out the punishments: the standard spankings, being sent to our bedroom without dinner, and we were often the recipient of a good belt whipping. However, once my father was gone for good, it all fell on my mother, causing an increase in her emotional fits of rage. She would explode in anger at the slightest infractions. If one or more of us were scurrying around and not in bed, she would have all of us line up in the living room and stand on one foot to tire us out. After what seemed like hours, with the little ones crying and begging her to stop, we would be sent back to bed. If it was for something really bad, she would spank us all one at a time, using belts and wooden yardsticks, and we older children would even get the chain-linked leashes used for her German shepherds. She walked behind us slowly, not knowing what she would use or who she would strike next.

She usually directed her efforts to the four oldest, Butch, Toni, Laurie, or me. Butch and Toni often got the worst of it. Butch was the tallest and always placed by the piano at the far end of the living room. My mother learned to play the piano at a young age and became quite good at it. Later, it became a marker in the room for where to stand for our beatings. She lined us up by age and height as she strode behind us like a drill sergeant, ready to smack anyone who spoke, giggled, or even let out a smirk. After a while of this routine, Butchy and I became more interested in finding humor in her erratic behavior, and would glance at each other, give each other a quick smile, or say something under our breath to anger her. We became used to the hits, and even though they would hurt for a bit, it was worth watching her become increasingly enraged at basically nothing. We were just kids doing what kids do.

However, I admit there were times when we deserved a spanking. Like when we destroyed the old trailer we lived in before moving into the big house. It sat empty on the property for many years. Following Butch's lead, we imitated Daniel Boone by throwing knives and axes into the thin wallpapered walls. She, in turn, beat us like never before and took an ax to Butchy's new bicycle, which was his prize possession, the only way for him to escape the property and, thus, the hell.

Another time we got some really big boxes of matches with a large striking abrasive on the side of the box. We began "innocently" lighting little fires a few feet away from each other. Butch was probably ten or so at the time, and being much younger, I looked up to him as my older brother. This isn't to say that I was innocent, as I gladly went along and struck up some matches with one of my older sisters, although they both deny it. I think there were just the three of us who didn't realize what would happen. Behind the prefab house there were large grass areas, but it was late summer, and the dry grass would light instantly. We incorrectly thought the small fires would all burn together in one area and we could contain them. However, we quickly discovered they were expanding outwards and beyond our control. Someone called the fire department to extinguish the large fire jeopardizing several buildings, including the abandoned home we grew up in, and even the Larrabee house next door. It was extremely fortunate that there was a firehouse right across the street, and no damage to any buildings.

Butch, the oldest boy and very rebellious by this time, seemed to get the brunt of my mother's rage. He was probably the one out of us all who resented her the most, and ultimately had hate in his heart for her. He was kicked out of the house by sixteen, and soon enough, he was on his way to Vietnam. Like many others at the time, he came home with a drug problem and no job prospects. He struggled for several years, moving out to Ohio, resulting in us having little to no contact with him. Finally, he returned to New York, settled in a poor neighborhood in Schenectady, married a young girl with two small babies from a previous relationship, and they gave birth to a son of their own. I may have run into him a few times between graduating high school and joining the military myself; however, when I grew older, my family and I spent several years out in the Midwest working in the country clubs, and I never saw him again. My understanding is that he reached out to everyone for help and support, and shamefully, he was turned away numerous times, especially by the one person who should have been there for him, his mother. Yet, why would any of us think that after the way she treated us growing up, there would be any way she would be there to help us as adults? Finally, around 1990, after recently separating from his wife, Butchy put a shotgun under his chin and ended all his pain and suffering.

I'm sure we did not make it easy on my mother. We were not the most well-behaved bunch. There was no denying that we had our own emotional issues, with the only physical contact that any of us kids received being through whips and spankings. It didn't help that we lacked proper supervision and leaned toward being a bunch of wild, delinquent kids. Many of our weekly, if not daily, spankings or beatings often came due to very insignificant infractions, and we never knew what precipitated them. Other times, we knew what was coming based on our actions. The more our life became intolerable, the more we rebelled and did really stupid and unbelievable things, hoping we could get away with it, or subconsciously wanting attention to get back at our mother, or both.

At this time, my mother found herself alone, with no job and little financial support from my father. To provide for her family, she had no choice other than filing for welfare. For a few years, the assistance was helpful, even if it was leftover military staples from the war. We were all too young to understand the dichotomy of living in one of the largest properties in the area, yet we needed government subsidies so we could eat. We were just thankful because it was food we couldn't get on our own. The government provided us with a safety net for all the necessities for a family, including loaves of bread and large five-pound tubs of peanut butter with the oil an inch thick on the top, which you had to stir up before use. In addition, they gave us three-pound blocks of cheese along with a cheese slicer, pancake mix, frozen sliced meats, similar to Steak-Umm, and canned meats like Spam; all good stuff, except for the powdered milk with probably zero butterfat that had to be mixed with water, and tasted disgusting. Sometimes the deliveries lasted a month, and sometimes they didn't. However, we got used to it, and although I was too young to understand why we were eating this way, we were thankful we had something.

Toni, the eldest, acted as our provider in many ways. She was responsible for watching us and feeding us as much, if not more often, than our mother. Toni would make pancakes, which we always seemed to have plenty of, and served us dinner quite often, washing the meals down with that government milk.

Despite my mother relying on Toni to care for us most of the time, their relationship only worsened when us younger siblings went to live with my father. Only seventeen at the time, Toni was beaten badly and thrown out of the house with only a suitcase. Walking down the highway late at night, crying, Toni wondered where she would go and what she would do. That was the last I saw of her for over a dozen years. She later confided in me that she went through a very difficult time, struggling to survive in a vibrant city. But she was a survivor, and with the help of friends and her church, she married and had three children that she ultimately ended up raising on her own. Butchy left around the same time and ended up in Vietnam.

Growing up poor meant that we often had to go to school in dirty clothes and without lunch, not even a sandwich. The schools did not have a federally funded program for lunches at that time, so if you did not have lunch in a bag or a cute, much-envied lunchbox, you would skip lunch, justifying it by saying that you had forgotten it at home, or telling the lie that I often used of "not really hungry today." At some point, I decided that the canned fruits and jellies in the cold cellar still had to be good enough to eat. They had to be edible, right? Wasn't that the purpose of canning and preserving? Wasn't that the purpose of those Ball jars, with a tight clamp sealing shut the lid of the jar on the pink rubber gasket, or the jellies and preserves that were topped with paraffin wax, a metal lid, and rubber seal before setting in boiling water to force out air and seal the contents? I remember my siblings and me checking them in the cellar to ensure they tasted okay. After a while of "not being hungry" at lunch, I decided on the days when I did not have any lunch to bring, I would bring a Ball jar of fresh pears, applesauce, or maybe a jar of jam in a paper bag. The other kids definitely stared at me inquisitively, followed by some smirks and giggles, but in my mind, I felt special because I had something no one else had—a feast for a king. More importantly, in hindsight, everyone saw that I was eating. On those days, I was no longer the poor kid sent to school without lunch.

The Lucky One

Growing up, there were many days when we became too much of a burden for my parents, especially when my mother was in the hospital. Gram would take care of us as much as she could; however, with her busy work schedule, we kids were sometimes pawned off onto any available relatives. I remember aunts and uncles who I wasn't very familiar with coming over during this period to help keep up with the house. There was a time when Uncle Robert's first wife, Audrey, who had two young boys of her own, came over daily while my mother was hospitalized, and helped with dinner and schoolwork. I am unsure if there was a schedule or rotation for whose turn it was to watch which kids, but for whatever reason, I always went with my Aunt Lois and Uncle Bill. I was about four years old when I started spending time with them, and it continued until my parents divorced. I never understood why I was the lucky one who got to go with them for all those years, but I never complained or spoke of anything when I returned, so as not to ruin a good thing.

Aunt Lois, my mother's aunt, and her husband, Uncle Bill, were a lovely middle-aged couple. He worked at General Electric in Schenectady during its heyday and, after a long career, was financially secure and lived a modest life in Glenville. They lived in a brick house about halfway down a short dead-end street. Their backyard went deep, giving their cocker spaniel and me plenty of room to run and play. I was so young when I started spending time with them. They would frequently pick me up and take me to their house for weeks, maybe months, when not in school. I think it could have even been the entire summer. As I grew older, the visits were fewer, but I felt like I had won a prize vacation with every visit. The difference between my two lives was stark, and even at my young age, I recognized that there was a better life, or at least a much different life out there. The perfect little house had pictures of their three children hung on the wall going up the stairs. In their living room was a beautiful modern cabinet, with a top that lifted to access a record player and doors in front that, when closed, hid the television.

Uncle Bill was a very large and rugged man, proud of the life he had built. He loved his family and friends, had a good job, and had no complaints. They had three children: Linda, Susan, and Bill Jr. They were teenagers when I started visiting, so there was an obvious age gap between us, which resulted in some awkward tension. One time, Bill Jr. was extremely upset when he learned that his mother let me play with his Erector Set. I can still hear him yelling, "Why does he have to touch my stuff? He's too young for an Erector Set." Aunt Lois reminded him that I was only visiting and needed toys to play with. Eventually, Bill Jr.'s feelings about me blew over, and he allowed me to use it. I'd never had such a wonderful toy, and I quickly became obsessed with making Ferris wheels and working cranes down in their basement.

Aunt Lois was not afraid of discipline; however, she had a way of doing it properly, supportively, without any physical beatings. This one time, we walked to the nearby grocery store, cutting across the neighbor's backyard and through a church parking lot to avoid walking on the main road. When we got home, she saw that I had taken a tube of toothpaste she had not paid for. It had a Pez dispenser attached to it with the word "FREE" on it. I didn't realize that the Pez dispenser was free if you bought the toothpaste, so she walked me all the way back to the store so I could hand the dispenser directly to the store manager and apologize. I definitely learned my lesson, but more importantly, I learned from my mistake without being spanked with a belt. When I was a bit older, we would stop at the little hobby shop, and she would buy me a model car that had to be put together, often with lots of pieces, that kept me occupied. In the late fifties, USS Nautilus was the first submarine to travel to the North Pole. From there, it continued underwater and emerged northeast of Greenland. I was so excited and thankful to my Aunt Lois for buying me the replica to build. It was one of my first plastic models, with over a hundred pieces that needed to be held together with very strong-smelling glue. I worked tirelessly on it at their small kitchen table, and I was beaming with such joy and a sense of accomplishment when I finally finished it. I'll never forget my Aunt Lois watching me build that toy model with love and encouragement. Since then, I have always been attracted to the smell of that model glue.

Aunt Lois and Uncle Bill were very social, too. Keno was popular back then, so the neighbors would get together for "game night." The kids would all go to one of the couple's houses, where an older kid would babysit as the adults played cards and enjoyed a few cocktails. They were also active boaters with a huge cabin cruiser that we would take up to Lake George. We would take the boat out and camp on the islands during the summer. Lake George is a spectacular, elongated lake with hundreds of tiny islands. Camping on the islands was quite popular, and we had to reserve spots with the park service. This included an appropriate size dock and water depth to accommodate larger boats, picnic spots with fire pits, and spacious open areas where we would set up the tents. Over the years, Aunt Lois and Uncle Bill developed friendships with the other boaters they met, and we would all reserve spots at Sand Island. The nights up on Lake George were very quiet and peaceful. The only sound I remember is the crackling wood in the fireplace and the rocking boat banging up against the buoys in the dock, with water slapping the rocks. At night, I heard faint music or the muffled laughter of other campers across the lake. Aunt Lois and Uncle Bill loved to listen to the local country western station, WGNA, which played traditional western songs by old timers like Johnny Cash and Conway Twitty.

The life I lived when I was with my aunt and uncle had a significant impact on me during those very impressionable years. I'll never understand why I was the only one sent with them, without any of my siblings. We always communicated with ourselves as a group but did not often share our feelings and emotions. So why was I the lucky one? I tucked away the guilt I felt of enjoying every minute I spent with my aunt and uncle, safe from the life I lived at home with my mother. Somehow, I knew I was different from the others. Maybe because I was the middle child, but it was more a feeling that I did not belong.

Freemans Bridge Road

After my father and mother split for good, my grandmother moved out of the apartment at the Big House and into her own two-story house outside of Scotia, which she rented from a former colleague. It was a lovely house with a full two-car garage. She decorated it with the nicest furnishings she purchased while working at the furniture store. Soon after, she married a long-haul trucker named Raymond Scawthorn, whom she met through his deliveries to the furniture store where she worked. Ray was a quiet, soft-spoken man. He must have had some good qualities for my grandmother to be attracted to him; however, we could never figure out what exactly they were. We all saw him as he was, a raging alcoholic, drinking brown liquors warm straight from the bottle—no need to add any ice or mixers. The only purpose of drinking for him was to prevent him from sobering up even a little. He was a WWII veteran who flew combat missions in the Pacific. After the war, he made a nice living driving eighteen-wheel tractor-trailers before he could no longer handle the long-haul trips. He retired and spent the rest of his life drinking himself to death. Other than that, we did not know much about him.

My grandmother tried for years to limit his drinking, but nothing worked, and eventually, he just sat for hours in the same metal chair with plastic-covered seats, drinking and looking out the window. Then he would sleep and wake up to do it all over again. His elbows were callused because he leaned on the table in the same position whenever awake. He would sit there for hours, reading every book written by the prolific western writer Louis L'Amour, watching TV, or drinking. My grandmother would throw out partial liquor bottles and hide money before going to work. He would just call a friend who drove a taxi to bring him a bottle, and if he didn't have any money, he would give the driver a radio or something of value that was my grandmother's. During this time, we remained with my mother at the Big House but would often go to stay at Gram's new place. We would beg, and Gram would negotiate with my mother to let us stay over. Unless we were being punished, my mother wouldn't balk at the opportunity of getting rid of one or all of us.

As times grew tougher, my mother decided she needed income, and the easiest way to do so was renting out our rooms at the Big House. This meant we had to move into the downstairs of Gram's two-story house with her husband Ray. They moved upstairs which had a small kitchen and a separate outside entrance. It was nice, but much smaller than we were used to. There were only two bedrooms, so my mother set up bunk beds in a small pantry off the kitchen, and one of us slept in a small den off the living room. I am still unsure why my Gram offered to help my mother out this way, especially after she and my father split. I assume it is because my grandmother would do anything to ensure we were safe and near. She was only looking to help us kids out, not my mother. Despite the turmoil we faced while living with my mother, there was such a comfort in knowing Gram was right upstairs.

Despite the comforting presence of Gram, my childhood memories are few and far between. I know I bounced around schools for most of my younger years. All I remember during my elementary years was going from school to school, feeling inferior, and never speaking to anyone, including the teachers, let alone classmates. I probably wasn't as silent or isolated as I remember. Still, I struggle to remember much of my childhood, except for a few situations and many of the bad times that seem to be etched in my memory. I remember one day at Sacandaga Elementary School when I was picked up by my arm, with my feet never touching the floor, and being carried to the principal's office for melting a whole box of Crayola crayons on the old steam radiator at the end of the hall, which was under a big window looking out to the playground. The radiators in the northeast back then were huge, and about four or five feet tall. I'm not exactly sure why, but I just stood there watching the crayons, one by one, dripping down the radiator until it was covered with a shitload of colors all dripping down the front. So, they called my mother to come to pick me up, only to turn me over to her. I'm sure she was extremely upset, but didn't show it at the school, so they wouldn't suspect that she was about to beat me silly as soon as we got home, if not in the car.

Another vivid memory in elementary school was the day all the teachers left their classrooms together and sobbed unapologetically in the hallway as they listened to the radio and the news that President Kennedy had just been shot in Dallas, Texas. Or the time one of my classmates went home one day from school and found her father had committed suicide in their garage and died of carbon monoxide poisoning, and how we all learned the details without even understanding the effects. Then, of course, I remember the "mandated" vaccinations that every child had to have in public school. We would line up, and the nurse would jab us with a needle or feed us a sugar cube for polio one by one. Tuberculosis was special, using a large drill-shaped tool with several tiny needles that, in most cases, left us all with a circular mark on our upper arm. But parents didn't get a choice in this and were thankful it was done at school, and everyone did not have to go to the doctor individually.

Then, of course, who could forget the atomic bomb drills: getting under the desks or kneeling in the hallways against the walls with our hands covering our heads, like that would have helped us in a nuclear attack? And there was that one day when my teacher received a note that I was to be excused, and my mother was on the way to pick us up from school. In typical fashion, Ray was so drunk that he had passed out upstairs; however, this time, he had a lit cigarette dangling from his mouth. As he slept, that cigarette fell, setting the entire upstairs on fire. Luckily, the fire department extinguished the fire before it spread downstairs, but there was still smoke and water damage. My grandmother's belongings, nice clothing, shoes, and furnishings still showed water and smoke damage years later. Gram was infuriated with him but was stuck, so she and Ray moved back downstairs, and my mother was forced to move us all back to the Big House.

So, what does that tell you? My only school memories were being scared to death of a potential nuclear bomb, two dramatic deaths, leaving early because our house caught on fire, being carried upside down to the principal's office, and preparing for another beating when I got home. This was a very emotional period of my life. The lack of consistency and emotional insecurity was more damaging than I could have ever imagined. No wonder I struggled in school. I changed schools at least six times within two years, causing me to be held back and have to repeat fifth grade. Added to the unstable home life, verbal and physical abuse, and severe social anxiety, it's amazing that I remember much of anything from these early years.

Rabbits

As a young kid, I would find anything to distract me from the rest of my world. I guess this was where my entrepreneurial drive began. I started stealing bottles from the Pepsi bottling plant next door to my grandmother's house to get some extra cash. Pepsi would discard bottles with any imperfections, so I would sneak over, take as many as I could, and return them to the store for deposit. With the money I scored, I was able to purchase a rabbit and cage being sold on the side of the road. Little did I know that soon after, raising rabbits would become my new obsession.

Behind the house was a free-standing two-car garage. There were small windows on all sides, work areas in the back, and a cellar with steps that went down about five or six feet to the dirt below the foundation. I'm assuming the original owners had chickens, because an upper shelf went around the entire space, perfect for my rabbit cages. Unsurprisingly, one rabbit soon became two, then three, and eventually, I had a dozen adult rabbits. It quickly became my hobby, and I spent all my time and energy learning the different varieties of rabbits and taking excellent care of them, with the sole purpose of breeding and selling them. I was sure that if I bought one on the side of the road, others would too.

My favorite was my first one: a black and white rabbit, fluffy with gorgeous black and white markings. It could have been a Dutch or Belgian Hare. I also had a pure white one with pink eyes, a light gray one with floppy ears, and some domesticated brown hares. I loved holding each one and talking to them—they were gentle and only scratched occasionally. Soon, I had a few of each different breed and focused on learning about their mating timelines and how large their litters would be. I wanted the most out of each litter, so what could be easier than putting males and females together? Rabbits are known to produce many offspring very rapidly. It did not take long before I had sixty rabbits consisting of several litters, strategically timed at different intervals so they could provide a steady stream of revenue for my little bunny enterprise.

I have to wonder: was my motivation to breed rabbits created to emulate my mother as she bred her German shepherds? We had watched for years as my mother bred her dogs and made money selling the pups. She had two beautiful purebred white German shepherds, which were rare and could be sold at a higher profit. I never gave it much thought at the time, but now I wonder if my "bunny business" was just me grasping at any common interest that my mother and I could share.

On Gram's property there was a doghouse between two very large pine trees. The dogs were always chained inside a large fenced-in area with grass so worn down it was almost nonexistent. The house sat on a busy highway, with thick woods in the back, so my mother would rarely let the dogs loose unless they were watched closely or held on leashes.

One day, I was following my usual routine of looking after the rabbits. I fed them, refreshed the waters, and cleaned their cages. When I finished, I let the rabbits out to mingle and exercise on the straw I had laid down on the dirt floor. I never let them out for long, but I knew they liked exploring the cellar. I had only made it back to the house for a few minutes before my heart sank. I heard my mother screaming for her dogs to return inside their fenced-in area. I rushed out of the house and ran to the back of the garage. I ran as fast as I could; however, in my heart, I feared the worst. I held my breath and flew down the cellar steps, but the damage had already been done. The rabbits were all dead, even the babies. Those damn dogs had a field day. They didn't eat them, but rather chased them, grabbed them by the necks, and shook them until each and every one was lifeless. It happened so quickly, like a tornado ripping through, leaving nothing on the ground but limp bodies and a blanket of fur.

What are the chances that she let her dogs loose at the same moment I didn't close the cellar door? Or worse, did she realize the door was up? I never thought that it was her fault at the time, and I believe it had little to do with my not speaking to her for over forty years, but in retrospect, maybe I did subconsciously blame her. She was quick to blame me at the time, snapping, "YOU left the door up while they were out of their cages. Don't blame the dogs—they can't help it—it's in their blood to hunt and kill rabbits!" Her opportunity to show me empathy and compassion was squashed as she beamed with pride over her canine hunters.

I knew that trying to place any of the blame on her would have been a bigger mistake, so out of fear, I said nothing. My heartbreak mixed with anger as she continued to yell at me, "Now, you have a mess down there, so get it cleaned up!"

I trudged down the cellar steps with a shovel and some old boxes. I could hardly see as my eyes welled with tears. At the time, they were my everything; now, they were all dead. I buried the boxes deep in the woods behind the garage, so the dogs couldn't sniff them out. However, it wouldn't have surprised me if they had found them. The author Vivian Shaw once wrote, "I find that if you dig deep enough you can almost always find something worth the effort."

Even though I secretly cried for weeks, I refused to show my mother how devastated I was over losing my rabbits. This moment certainly wasn't the first time she could not display any sense of compassion, empathy, or emotion toward me. However, this might have been the moment when I realized that she loved her prize shepherds more than me.

Social Services

Even though it was the mid-sixties, a single mother with seven children living on government assistance meant the county had its eyes on us. Despite not being religious by any means, my mother was convinced by a friend to join the local Mormon church. She thought if it looked like we were a happy, churchgoing family, social services wouldn't have any reason to take us from her. So, we began attending Sunday service regularly. That church had a small pool to the right of the altar, with steps on both sides to walk in and out of. Before we knew it, we were each placed in robes, a few at a time, and were baptized in front of the entire congregation. Unbeknownst to any of us, we were now on the Mormon rolls in Salt Lake City...for life.

However, all her efforts were futile. My mother must not have realized that moving from house to house and having to enroll and disenroll in schools so frequently within a short period, all while still maintaining government assistance, caused some serious red flags. "Say anything bad to the social services people—you will never see your brothers and sisters again!" my mother threatened Toni, as Social Services came to evaluate our living situation and family life. Ultimately, the county believed we were better off being placed in the care of the Pogorzelskis, a foster family who lived in Delanson. This meant we changed schools yet again and now attended Duanesburg Elementary. I don't remember much of this place, but I know we were safe and cared for. The Pogorzelskis were very lovely people. They lived in a large sprawling farmhouse that seemed to have several additions as they took in more and more families. They had their own children, so the house was chaotic now, adding us. Mrs. Pogorzelski was in a wheelchair suffering from ALS. I believe they took on fostering to receive money from the county, but that didn't take away from the fact that they chose to take in strangers' children and did the best they could with support and affection while it was determined where would be the best place for us. Best of all, I still got to spend the summer with Aunt Lois and Uncle Bill.

After about nine months, the county temporarily returned custody to my mother—although I am sure they questioned their decision. "Who would you prefer to live with?" I remember being asked while interviewed by the family court judge. "Your mother or your father?" It was as if my mother made us rehearse our responses. "You tell them you want to go to St. Colman's with your cousins!" she had said, desperate for us to go anywhere but back with our father. St. Colman's was a large facility run by the Catholic church for abandoned children and families of broken homes. This was where Aunt Margaret's children, Walt, Marie, and Terry, went. I'm sure it wouldn't have seemed the worse choice then; however, the school was investigated years later, after decades of accusations of sexual abuse.

After much questioning, the family court placed us in the custody of the county, and the five of us were sent to the Schenectady County children's home—the last stop for children of broken homes before adoption. The hope was that this would only be a short-term solution until social services determined the best for all involved. The building was a three- or four-story, old brick structure halfway down Union Street in Schenectady. While living there, we were restricted to the small "compound," and would be escorted by the shelter workers back and forth from school, never going anywhere else. I began another school year at another new school—Schenectady Elementary in the Stockade area of Schenectady, within walking distance of the shelter. I still remember enjoying the walk to school each day. The Stockade was rich in history as it was one of the oldest neighborhoods in the city, dating back over three hundred years. On February 8th, 1690, the French military raided the Stockade, destroying the homes and community of over sixty residents. There is a statue of "Lawrence," a Mohawk Native American who encouraged the Dutch to resettle the village after the attack. I will never forget walking past that statue almost every day while we waited to hear our fate. He was the community's symbol of life after darkness, and hope for the future.

I have to say, the staff at the shelter were charming and compassionate. I know they did their best to ensure we all felt safe and secure, with a bit of normalcy in our lives. I still remember the bedrooms on the second floor having steel bars on the windows, complete with ten-foot fencing around the property to ensure we did not jump out of a window and try to escape, although we had no reason to. We were treated well, attended school regularly, and were consistently fed.

Even though we may have only been there for just a few months, I will never forget the sounds of my siblings crying themselves to sleep at night as I stared out through the bars of the windows at the bright autumn moon. Yes, I also wanted to cry, but I refused. Not being wanted was nothing new; truthfully, most of the crying was beaten out of me before I was ten. It was just the unknown that made me tear up. The adoption of five siblings was unheard of, especially for children ranging from four to twelve years of age. Undoubtedly, we would have been split up, with the younger siblings being adopted, while we older ones were sent to various foster homes or even worse, St. Colman's, until we were old enough to live independently. In any event, there was no chance we would have been kept as one unit and would have unquestionably been separated for good.

One night, as I waited to fall asleep until I knew my siblings had, I stared out that small window, and I couldn't help but wonder how we were utterly abandoned. I knew my mother didn't want us any longer, but where was our father? Where was Gram? Everyone who knew and supposedly loved us—how could they let us sit here by ourselves? My body heated up with anger as my frustrations with my family grew. I recall one very kind social worker, probably in her early twenties, who took a liking to all of us. She was a young, attractive Polish gal from the Cobleskill area. She would work the night shift to get us all into bed. I'll never forget her soft, compassionate voice saying, "Life will get better. Everything is going to be okay." I just stared out that window as I wiped away the tears that rolled down my cheek.

Christmas

The clatter of dishes as Kim cleared away Christmas brunch broke into my childhood memories. As much as I was grateful to my wife for keeping in touch with my siblings, the tension in my body remained. Spending time with them meant those old feelings would resurface. I tried to relax. Courtney licked cinnamon roll frosting from her fingers and suggested a game of Monopoly, so the boys followed her into the living room, while I stacked the last of the plates and joined Kim in the kitchen.

But as the gathering got closer, the tightness in my neck and chest escalated. When the day came, and everyone started to gather at our house, I hid in the kitchen like I often did, while Kim, more comfortable with small talk, greeted my family. The party always consisted of all five of my sisters and my little brother, their children and now their children's children, and my Aunt Donna and Ronnie, her husband of over fifty years. My father was included before he passed away many years ago. In fact, this tradition began when my father and his new wife, Carol, began inviting us over to swap gifts and see each other around the holiday. Needless to say, even when my mother lived locally, she was never included.

Some of the clan came through the front door, past my landscaping smothered in white, twinkly lights. Others cut through the garage. They all brought their traditional dishes to complement whatever proteins I cooked that year. Everyone looked forward to Uncle Bill's Prime Ribs of Beef. The kitchen smelled increasingly like Christmas, the aroma wafting into the other rooms to blend with the appropriate holiday-scented candles and soft holiday music by one of my wife's favorite crooners. The chatter of everyone greeting each other increased as they discussed where to hang the coats and where to put the food and drinks that they brought. It was customary for Debbie and her husband Larry to run late, upset at something her kids did or just nervous that no one would like her potatoes. She is my closest, dearest sister, since we are only eleven months apart; we also share many emotional traits like anxiety and insecurity. Despite her attempts to put on a happy face, I could always tell she was having just as hard of a time at these gatherings as me.

"Merry Christmas, honey," I softly told Debbie as I gave her an extra big hug and kiss. "How ya doing?" I've always been especially concerned for her. Being so much alike, I believe I understand her better than most. Because we were in the same grade in school, we would see each other often in the hall. She was quiet, with only a few genuine friends. I got involved with sports, so I was looped into different crowds, but I always kept an eye on her.

"I'm good," she said unconvincingly. But, of course, she should have known by now that her forced smile wouldn't work on me.

Debbie is shorter than most of us, with brown, shoulder-length hair. She is the most selfless, kind person, and we all know she would do anything for her family, friends, and their children. But, unfortunately, like me, her glass is often half empty, and she never could embrace the joy in life without effort.

The noise level rose as another group arrived, and the background music was hardly distinguishable. The kitchen island became the party's center, where hors d'oeuvres were served and drinks poured. This made it very difficult for me to finish the cooking as everyone congregated around the food, cornering me by the stove as if by some unexplained gravitational force. Each year, I say I'm going to cordon off my space with yellow police tape.

It's hard to say that we all haven't dealt with some level of PTSD from our childhood trauma—how could we not? I cannot speak on behalf of my siblings, as we each internalize our experiences differently; however, I do know that my upbringing has left me with many emotional scars that continuously seep into my family, friendships, and work relationships. Ever since my panic attack at the chance to be the center of attention on the Freddie Freihofer show, I have lived with a constant fear of being judged, mixed with debilitating self-esteem and phobia of public speaking. I despise social situations and have learned to cope throughout my career by overcompensating with other strengths to prove, in some way, that I am worthy.

After what seemed like an eternity, the party finally began to wind down, and everyone started packing up children and leftovers. As per usual, I had cooked way too much, and there was plenty for my sisters to take home with them. With each goodbye, I exhaled a bit more, and my shoulders dropped a few inches as I finally started to relax. I made sure that I was able to say goodbye to Debbie. "Smile! I love you," I told her as I hugged her hard. There was such a comfort between the two of us. Our smiles might have been forced, but our hug was sincere and just what we both needed.

The holiday hustle and bustle continued for days with parties, dinners, and genuine, warm family time. Billy caught a flight back to Las Vegas a few days after Christmas, and Kim, Courtney, and I worked various parties together at the club for New Year's Eve. We were wiped out by New Year's Day, but it was time to pack up Christmas and clean up those last gifts lying around. I fooled myself into thinking I was in control, but my wife and daughter were calling the shots, and they had decided about this whole DNA thing.

"Come on, just spit in the tube already and send it back," my wife instructed me with a friendly nudge. "The tests are expensive; Courtney paid a lot for that gift. Come on, make your daughter happy. She'll be disappointed if you don't do it." Kim pushed the box into my chest because my hands were full of the tubs filled with our ornaments, tucked carefully away for next year's gathering.

When I got up the next day, Kim had already left the house to meet her sister for lunch. I saw that DNA kit, where my wife had left it, right in the middle of the center island in the kitchen, where I couldn't miss it. Between Kim and Courtney, I knew I would not know a moment's peace until I spit into the tube. So, I opened the box and did what I was told, popped the kit in the mail, and forgot all about it.

Valentine's Day

Before we knew it, Valentine's Day was upon us. Kim and I were in bed having our morning coffee. I have brought my wife her coffee in bed every morning for nearly thirty-six years. I love this ritual before heading into the stress of our jobs. We have these peaceful, blissful moments together at the top of each day to sip our coffee, check our emails, see what "fires" we might have to put out when we get to work, and spend a few moments connected to one another.

"My DNA results have come back," I said, feeling a lurch in my stomach. I hadn't expected to feel this apprehensive. I sat straight up in bed and opened the email from Ancestry.com. I didn't get far scrolling before Kim grabbed my laptop (she had already figured out how to navigate the site) to see my results.

"Yup, I knew it! You're fifty percent Italian!"

I laughed outwardly, but inside, I was rattled. *How on earth am I Italian?* I felt uneasy, as I realized that somebody hadn't been completely honest with me about who I was and where I came from.

"I guess we should have realized that since Billy was twenty-six percent Italian, I would be fifty percent, or you would have some explaining to do," I said with a chuckle, lightening the mood. But something was nagging at me about this, and now I had to get to the bottom of it. My family had pried open the Pandora's box of my background, and that had always been a daunting proposition.

The more I thought about it, the more my mind was swirling with questions I could not answer. Nothing made sense about this, and now, we would be late for work. I tried to clear my mind and focus on my day ahead. This was something I took pride in as a manager. I could always close the door on my personal life and continue with my work for the day with a level head, free of distractions. Until now. Kim and I agreed to put the whole matter aside for the moment, yet the minute we got home from work, we were back at the computer running through any explanation we may have missed.

"Well, I'm glad at least Billy knows who *his* father is!" I told my wife, as she was cooking dinner that night. She chuckled as she threw the ingredients into a bowl, making my favorite meatloaf.

"What is so funny?" I asked, finding nothing of this situation humorous. But then she asked me an unbearably strange question. Strange, because I could never have imagined that I would have to answer it: "What would be worse—your father is not your father or your son is not your son?" she asked. She obviously knew my answer, but also provided a little comic relief to this heavy and nauseating situation.

"Of course, that my son is not my son!" I said sharply. Even though I found her question annoying, I was thankful to have Kim through this. Between her and Billy, they filled in all my shortcomings, brought me back to reality, paid attention to detail, and observed every connection listed, trying to make sense of this situation.

"So, Jeff's daughters do show up as your nieces. Although they don't show any Italian in their DNA," she said curiously. She remembered seeing that everything matched the other half of my DNA, which was on my mother's side but showed no Italian. At this point, all I could do was pace around our kitchen island, picking things up and putting them back down without thinking. My body was moving unconsciously as my brain worked on overdrive.

Jeff was the spitting image of my father, from his facial features to his mannerisms and even the sound of his voice. There was no question about who his father was. My stomach churned, and my heart, which now felt like the weight of ten cinder blocks, sank lower into my gut.

Kim slid her meatloaf into the oven, washed her hands, and returned to the computer. With some quick clicks, she ended up back on the Ancestry site.

"Wait. Who is this Ricky guy from Indiana? He shows up almost as close a match as Billy! Could he be a half brother you didn't know about?" she asked.

"No idea," I replied. "Maybe my father spent time in Indiana that we didn't know about? Or that guy's mother spent time in New York and had a relationship with my father?"

We had our dinner, but we both couldn't stop thinking about this crazy shit dumped on me. We continued to ask questions or bounce crazy ideas off each other, but always ended with an "Oh yeah" or "That couldn't be." Finally, we fell asleep, each waiting for the other to mumble something enlightening.

Falling in Love

It may seem cliché, but it was love at first sight when I met Kim on my first day at my job as executive chef at The Edison Country Club. Kim had been their banquet coordinator for a year when I arrived in my new position. This meant that we would be working closely together every day. I ran the kitchen and back of house while she managed the dining room and events. It's common in this business for flirtatious relationships to brew between men in "back of house" and women who work "front of house."

Kim was—and still is—a stunningly beautiful woman with straight medium-length blond hair above her collar. Even in her old photos from the sixties and seventies, when long hair was all the rage, she kept hers shorter. Standing five foot ten, she carries herself with elegance and class and is always surrounded by such a sense of confidence. I wasn't just smitten; she was all I could think about morning, noon, and night, so finally, we had the opportunity to be alone after work one evening, sitting at the bar and having shift drinks. It was after our second cocktail when I made my move. My body felt hot, my legs shook, and I panicked, thinking this would only be a onetime thing. But, lucky for me, it was real, and we have been together ever since.

We soon moved into an apartment together, and before we knew it, we were expecting our first son. I was elated and began acting like a goofy new father, and she was radiant and poised as ever as a pregnant mother. I had dreamt of this my whole life: a family of my own. There was no way I was going to repeat any of my parents' failures.

The entire staff at the club was excited for us, and once our son was born, I couldn't wait to show him off. He had a huge head and was a unique shade of purple; to me, he was the prettiest baby born to date. I paraded proudly, showing everyone his tiny Polaroid picture probably many times. We named him William Joseph Aperance III, after my father, who was a junior named after his father. My middle name was different, as my mother wanted me to have a tribute to her Uncle Raymond, who was killed in World War II. I was initially upset when my older sister Laurie, who had her second son before I had my first, also named him William after my dad. To my insecure mind, this was not done. The father's name should always be reserved for the oldest son to have priority to use the name and carry on the namesake. Over the years, I realized how petty this was, and learned that it was my issue and not anything to remain mad at her for.

When Billy was just about eight months old, Kim and I decided to get married. We didn't have much money, and in 1984, married couples received *a lot* back when filing taxes, as opposed to filing as two singles. So, we packed the car, grabbed our social security cards and birth certificates, dropped Billy off with Grandma, and drove down to the "Jewel of New Jersey," Atlantic City, our car fueled by love and the hopes of a large tax refund. The secrecy and the fact that this beautiful woman was willing to be my wife were exhilarating. I was over the moon, knowing we really did love each other. My new life was propelling me farther away from my past.

Atlantic City was doing well at the time. The area was pretty run down until they started rebuilding the boardwalk with newer hotels and casinos with top entertainment to rival Vegas on the east coast. Neither of us had been to Vegas or even New York City, so it was thrilling. Upon arrival, we went straight to our hotel, checked in, and were eager to head to City Hall to complete the paperwork. We had some time so we took a quick walk taking in all the smells and sounds of the boardwalk and casinos. We stopped at a flower shop on the boardwalk. "Wait here!" I said as I ran in quickly, returning with a corsage of red roses and a hint of baby's breath. "I love you," I told her with a soft kiss on the cheek.

Inside City Hall, there was a massive entryway with the usual marble staircase going up either side to a second floor. We looked frantically for the clerk's office and walked in, with my arm still around her waist.

"We are here to get married!" I exclaimed, the words leaving my mouth drenched in excitement and, let's be honest, a lot of nerves. The attendant at the welcome desk directed us up to the second floor and the city clerk's office.

The lady at the counter handed us some paperwork and told us to complete it and bring it back to her. We found a spot to sit, and with my trembling hands, I filled out my portion and slid the documents across the table to Kim. Once our paperwork was completed, we jumped back up and hurried to the front desk as instructed, returning with our social security cards and birth certificates. She looked over everything and then peered over her glasses to ask us for one final requirement. At that moment, our hearts sank. We looked at each other in horror, unaware of this significant detail. I'll never forget how I felt when the woman asked, "And who will be standing up for you?"

Not getting married on this day was not an option. Not only did we drive this whole way, but it was after Christmas, and we wanted to make sure this happened before December 31st to claim our marriage for the whole year on our taxes.

"Wait here, and I'll be right back."

Kim awkwardly sat back down as I hurried down the hall and the long marble staircase, my brain rushing as fast as my feet as I scoured the lobby. I saw a man in blue overalls buffing the lobby floor. *He will do nicely,* I thought as I approached him, noticing his name embroidered above his right pocket.

"Hey...Mike, can you help me out for a minute?" I politely asked, and went on to explain our situation. Mike agreed out of the kindness of his heart (and the large bill passed during our handshake), and I led him back up the stairs and down the hall to the office where Kim was waiting. As we returned to the office, I said proudly, "Kim! Look who I ran into downstairs, our old buddy Mike!" The lady behind the counter cracked a smile and pointed to the location on the document that Mike had to sign. She then told us to wait in the hallway until the judge was available.

On December 27th, 1984, we were pronounced man and wife, as the judge on duty squeezed us in between a drunk driver and a domestic violence case. We took a picture with the judge and our "old buddy Mike," our only wedding photo. We thanked them both, and Mike returned to work downstairs with an extra day's pay in his pocket. That night, we had reservations at the Sands Hotel, one of the most extravagant spots on the strip. We enjoyed a lovely dinner and scored front-row seats to Sammy Davis Jr., which included a personal serenade once Mr. Davis Jr. realized we were newlyweds. Why else would Kim still be holding her rose with both of us beaming like we just won the jackpot in the casino?

My career at this time was advancing. The Edison Club had been going through a tough time with membership and financial stability. Kim and I were credited with turning the club into a profitable operation. After cleaning house with the current management, they promoted me to Club Manager and Kim to my assistant. Country clubs are much different animals in so many ways than any regular restaurant or hotel. The most significant difference is that the members are "owners" of the club, and even though they elect a board to oversee the operation and management, they all expect the staff to be friendly but subservient. Members utilize the club for rest and relaxation, and often dine with us three or four times a week. They use the facilities a great deal and have high expectations. It's their "home away from home." This meant that we had hundreds of bosses each day. Would they be happy with their meal? Was the building's temperature okay? Would the speed of play be to everyone's liking? Were there enough cushions available for the pool chairs? We never knew what each day would bring, so we always had to double our efforts to ensure their satisfaction and provide service commensurate with their annual dues. With each club I worked, the board supported my management style and success. I would take a fledgling club in fiscal and operational trouble, and, with the collaboration of my management teams and committee members, I looked to improve the quality of service, reduce expenses, and turn the club profitable. From the grounds crew to the kitchen staff, front-of-house employees, and everyone else, I did my best to ensure everyone went above and beyond and delivered the utmost service.

This didn't always come easy, however. In my earlier days as a young manager, I believed there was some benefit to striking fear into employees as a motivational tool. This was successful for me for many years, as our industry was still a rough environment—not yet a kinder world with labor, harassment, and sexual innuendo laws that were instituted later, making most of my management style unacceptable. When members heard me chastise an employee, they assumed I was doing a good job, and doing what they needed me to do.

The truth was, most of my aggression came from the fact that I went to work each day thinking it would be the day I would be let go. That the members would not be pleased with the direction the club was moving, and one of my many daily decisions would not be up to their standards, and I would be fired. With the fear of losing my job looming daily, I became instantly upset with anything I perceived would make me, or my operation, look bad.

My mentality was that I was the general manager, and everyone's choices were a reflection of me and my job. This only increased the pressure I felt each day. One minute, I would be a ray of sunshine and happily going about my business, and then, an unexplained wave of pessimism would come over me. Often, what someone may have said earlier that day or even days prior triggered this, but usually, by the time my feelings turned into anger, I was lashing out at anyone I came in contact with. There were times when Kim and I had a particular word or comment that was her signal for me to walk away, go to my office and stay put. Not always heeding her warning, I would continue my rampage and find who irritated me the most. Kim ended up being my frustration sounding board more times than I wish to say. I knew she could take my verbal ranting. I relied heavily on Kim's calm demeanor to help defuse situations and let me know if or when I was about to cross the line. She was also my interpreter for what was said during interactions and meetings, as my brain often only processed conversations with a negative, paranoid lens.

When we told people that we worked together, they always seemed shocked. Not only did we make it work, but it strengthened our relationship in many ways. We were fifty-fifty partners at work and home from day one. We got to see the best and worst of each other (even though there is hardly any fault to find in her). We complimented each other's strengths, sometimes playing a little "good cop, bad cop," yet for the most part, we had different responsibilities and could even go hours without seeing each other. She was responsible for booking all the social and member functions, and I oversaw club operations, including golf course, pool, tennis, financial budgeting, and facilities maintenance.

Anyone who knows this business can speak to the strain on relationships due to the long hours and unique situations that are virtually impossible to explain to a spouse with no understanding of it at all. Those who have a spouse not in hospitality can't fully understand when their partner may be on totally different work and sleep schedules. We were together twenty-four-seven.

Kim has always been a spectacular mother. She has a calm but matter-of-fact way of parenting. She would rock the children gently, reading stories to them each night. She loved taking them to the library, as money was tight in those days. They would spend hours in wide-eyed wonderment, selecting just the right books. Thanks to Kim's consistent effort to teach them to enjoy learning, all three children learned to love the library and were far ahead of their classmates in reading and writing.

We had the benefit of rotating our time away from the club to manage the kids, support their activities, help with homework, and attend school functions. We worked hard to make sure at least one of us was there. This wasn't always possible; we had a few steady babysitters, including Kim's mother, Linda, to help us with them.

So, the question is, why has she stayed with me and dealt with all my emotional issues for all this time? Many friends and family have wondered about this over the years, but I know that she genuinely loves me. Having learned all my secrets, my childhood trauma, and why I am who I am, she understands me. With her unshakable kindness and strength, she made me a better man.

I ultimately learned to overcome my frustrations in later years, and my outbursts became fewer and fewer. At the beginning of my career working in the kitchen, behind closed doors, it was like the Wild West—anything could be said and done behind the kitchen doors by a crude and irate chef with an ego the size of a walk-in cooler. I quickly transitioned to "front of house" behavior, running a dining room full of the upper echelons. My personality was not meant for that. Behind the kitchen doors, I did not have to engage with any members. I just made their food and hoped they enjoyed their meals. My only communication was when a waitress came back to report any feedback from their tables. Later, being out front led to daily interaction with people I never felt comfortable with. I grew up differently than they did. I was abandoned, abused, and neglected. I grew up drinking powdered milk and eating government cheese. I stole bottles on the side of the road just to earn a little money of my own. Who was I to think that I could manage an upscale country club?

I can say now that my management career was successful. Experts in our industry say an average general manager lasts about three to five years at one location. I was finishing my eighteenth year at Albany Country Club when I retired. Yet I'd be lying to say that all that success didn't come at a cost.

Inbox

Kim and I eventually fell asleep after our evening of exploring my ancestry, and it was morning before I knew it. I poured our coffee and jumped in the shower. We were both tired and had not gotten much sleep, but I felt an enormous amount of anxious energy. This whole nightmare was beginning to consume me. I fed Sadie, and left the house before Kim had finished getting ready.

Despite having offices next to one another, Kim and I often drove separately to work. This allowed me to leave when I finished for the day, as Kim often needed to stay until the end of parties and events. I arrived at work and made my rounds, pouring myself a fresh cup of coffee and sharing a "good morning" with the other employees. On a typical day, I would chat with the office ladies or our golf pro about the latest member musings. But today, I immediately went into my office, shut the door, and pulled up Billy's Ancestry account on my computer. Seeing my niece's DNA without Italian blood was just as frustrating as it was confusing. I was filled with a wild tornado of anxiety and obsession. Like a car crash, I couldn't look away. But instead of a vehicle, it was my life that was in pieces, thrown about the highway.

I quickly closed the website. *Why am I even bothering with this?* I thought. *I'm sixty-five years old and have spent the last half decade avoiding reliving my past. What would be the benefit of unearthing the unknown now? If it were true that my father was not my biological father, then how would this affect my family? What would this do to my siblings?* Just the thought of this alone made me sick, so I left my office to try to relax in the smokers' lounge with a cigar. When Kim arrived, she came downstairs to find me. "You must look into your connection with this Ricky Renschler guy in Indiana. You can't just ignore that." I took a long drag of my cigar, filling the small garage space with wafting smoke. I didn't look at her, but I knew she was right. I left my cigar balancing on the shelf, and we headed back upstairs. Everyone at the club knew when I was around by the distinct smell of my cigars, or by seeing the half-smoked stogie left in various crevasses around the basement.

We went into my office and pulled up the Ancestry site again. First, we confirmed that my nieces, Chrissy and Debbie, not only did not have any Italian, but even more distressing was that they were not even related to this unknown Ricky Renschler, a prominent figure in my connections. He only matched me and my son Billy, since no other family members had taken the DNA test at that time.

"You need to reach out to him!" Kim demanded. "He's the only clue you have right now."

"I know!" I snapped. "Just give me some time."

I decided to contact him through the Ancestry site. As I clicked around to find how to send a direct message, I saw his name already in my inbox, like he was waiting for me. Holy shit! I thought. He had already sent Billy a message over a year ago.

Billy would have never looked at the messages since he was only interested in his ancestry, quickly learning his and my wife's genealogy and never digging any deeper to see what connections there may have been on my side. He was not looking for anything unusual, and we shrugged off the twenty-six percent Italian at the time. He never went searching out any relatives for DNA matches. This was two years before even my nieces did their tests.

With shaky hands, I typed him a response. I introduced myself and explained that he had messaged my son.

This guy must have had his notifications on for the website to alert him of my message, because he got back to me quicker than a teenager on Snapchat. In his reply was his contact information. At this point, there was no going back, and I had to see if he had any answers to all these new questions that came flooding into my world, all because of my daughter's dumb Christmas gift.

If anyone had the answers, Ricky Renschler would. If he was a half brother to me, as indicated by the number of genetic matches we shared, then his father would be my father. *I will soon have those answers and learn who my biological father is.*

I was nervous as hell, my hands shaking as I dialed each number. "Hello?" he said with a midwestern drawl.

"Ricky, I'm William Aperance," I said. My stomach was still in knots, and now, my mouth became increasingly dry, making it more difficult to talk. "Looks like we might be related somehow..."

After the first few minutes of the call, I could tell he had been anxiously waiting to connect with me. He was easy to talk to, and I felt more at ease with him as he told me his story.

"I live in Evansville, Indiana, and was adopted as a baby by a wonderful couple," he explained. "They told me that I was adopted as a child, but it was just in the past few years that the state passed a law that allowed individuals to access their adoption records. I found out that my mother Joyce had given birth to me in 1958 at a home for unwed mothers. However, no father was listed on the birth certificate."

All my excitement and anticipation quickly vanished like the air rushing out of a balloon.

"I had taken the Ancestry test and found that we were somehow connected, and that's when I reached out to your son," he continued. "My wife and I also looked you up on Facebook and found your country club website."

I heard his wife, Cindy, in the background, joining in on the conversation. "I could tell you were brothers right away," she exclaimed.

We chatted for another half hour, going back and forth about who our parents were and where we lived growing up, and nothing could explain our connection. No one he knew was from New York, and no one I knew lived in Indiana. As it appeared that neither of us could make any sense of our history, we committed to continuing to research our connection, and agreed to speak again soon. I hung up the phone, more baffled and deflated than ever, and sat silently for about an hour. My office door was still closed, but I could hear people heading up and down the hallway, pushing carts and speed racks on and off the elevator, talking and laughing. Our maintenance man, Spencer, asked Kim if I was busy, and her quick response was, "He is on a business call."

I sat at my desk, frozen, the phrase "What the fuck" swirling in my head repeatedly. Kim quietly knocked and opened my office door, waiting to hear how the call went.

"Well, I have a half brother in Indiana..." I spoke matter-of-factly. Kim stood in the doorway, silent as I continued to spew questions that I knew she did not have the answers to. "Did I have an Italian father that moved to Indiana? Did he have another family? Do I have another family?"

"Ricky was adopted," I told her. "His mother gave birth in a home for unwed mothers, but the birth certificate had no father listed. So, we are definitely half brothers, but neither of us has the slightest idea who the fuck our father is! A fucking dead end," I barked.

I stood up out of my chair and went over to the window. I looked out to the parking lot and our meticulous practice facility. Of course, there was always a beautiful garden in the summer, but in late February in upstate New York, it looked cold and bleak. Kim made her way over to my computer, looking around the site for any more clues or connections. I stood in silence, wondering how on earth I could be connected to this man from Indiana.

"Michael Schermerhorn!" my wife shouted with excitement, breaking the painful silence that weighed in the room. "Isn't that Toni's son?" she asked.

"Yeah, but what is his connection to me?" I asked, beginning to doubt anyone I knew to be related to me anymore.

"He shows as your nephew and has a good amount of Italian in his DNA," Kim stated. "Could your mother have gotten back with her first husband? Butch and Toni's father? That could make perfect sense. When did she divorce him and marry your father?" She asked.

"I have no clue. I can text Debbie and ask her." I took my cell phone out of my pocket and texted my sister, my hands still clammy from the last call I had made. Debbie was the one who kept tabs on everyone and knew almost everything about our family.

Hey, honey! I texted. *Any chance you know the dates of our mother's divorce and when she married Dad?*

She texted back right away. *I'm not sure. But Laurie was born in '52, so it has to be '53, right? Why, what's up?*

Just curious, talk to you later, I texted back.

I didn't have the energy to bring her into the mix and break this news to her today. Especially since I hardly had any information to share, except that I have a half brother in the Midwest, and neither of us knows who our father is. I was in no mood to drop this wild bomb through text, but I knew we would have to have the conversation very soon.

My parents had constantly been fighting and separating from the early days, so it made perfect sense that my mother could have reconciled with Conti (or even just had a romp for old times' sake) in early 1954 when I was conceived.

We thought this was a very logical scenario, making Toni and Butch my full brother and sister, sharing identical DNA, and making me a half brother to my other three sisters and youngest brother. Mystery solved? Finding out that I had the same mother and father as my older sister and brother would not be upsetting to me in the least. Everything would be the same with my siblings except for awkward jokes at the next family get-togethers. When we were all growing up, we never considered them any different. We never called them "half"; we were all just brothers and sisters. So it would be no big deal, besides exposing the already known marital troubles and now my mother's infidelity.

I leaned on this scenario being the best case. However, the thought of my mother getting with some other Italian or a friend of Conti from that area of mostly Italian immigrants haunted me. Thinking that maybe it was some drunken, broken-down old deadbeat that never made anything of himself was very stressful. That would be my worst nightmare. Was I the son of a nobody?

I started thinking, *what if my grandmother screwed around with an Italian man and my father's father was not Lithuanian?* If this was the case, my grandfather didn't just "go out for a pack of cigarettes," never to return. Instead, he may have left her because she had an affair in the Bronx with an Italian. This would make me feel much better.

Toni and Butchy's father was a New York State Trooper back then, so for a day or two I hoped he was my father, thinking what a coincidence it would be since I wanted to be a trooper, and was a military policeman when in the service. He was a decent man, remarried with a family in Amsterdam.

Kim was still searching and cross-checking anyone who was a match to myself, my son, and Ricky. "Ricky...does not match Michael Schermerhorn," she said as a matter of fact. That eliminated the possibility that Toni and I shared the same father. Conti would have never traveled to Indiana while having another family in Amsterdam. As much as we hoped this was the end of the search, we kept running all the previous scenarios back and forth. The Lithuanian-Italian theory or mix-up was quickly dashed, because my younger brother Jeff's two daughters had taken the test by this point. They were listed as my nieces, matching my mother's heritage but showing zero Italian. This also cleared my grandmother of any hanky-panky, or my nieces would also have had Italian in their genes. and there was no way Jeff was not my father's son.

Kim called our son Billy as soon as we got home that night and updated him on the call with Ricky. We kicked around all these possibilities, and Billy quickly discounted them one at a time.

"It makes perfect sense that you're fifty percent Italian if I'm twenty-six percent," Billy said dispassionately. He did not get emotional over such things. Billy is a literal thinker with a wonderful way of breaking down complex issues so we can all understand them clearly. It was comforting in a strange sort of way, seeing the world through Billy's eyes.

"There are only three possible explanations for this," Billy said methodically. He had clearly thought this all through and was waiting for us to catch up.

"First scenario, your grandparents from Lithuania were both actually a hundred percent Italian, making your father a hundred percent Italian, making you fifty percent," he said.

Kim and I nodded our heads, waiting for Billy to continue.

"Second possibility, your grandmother conceived your father with an Italian and not with the Lithuanian husband who had left town when your father was a young boy." Kim and I looked at each other, astonished at this new version of our son as a genetic detective.

"Or finally, the elephant in the room, the father who raised you might not have been your biological father."

The pit in my stomach I had felt when I first opened my results started churning. Here I was, approaching sixty-five, and everything I'd ever known about *who* I was and where I'd come from was a lie. Questions were emerging about my life that I'd never even thought to ask. And all this had come from a tiny bit of curiosity, a desire to please my daughter and a small saliva sample. I felt very strange. These questions dominated my thoughts. All I could think about for weeks was, *Who am I? Who's my father? Was I adopted? Is that why I spent all that time with Aunt Lois and Uncle Bill when the others didn't?* Whatever the truth, now I had to find out.

We ran all the options again with Billy on speakerphone. He quickly shot down our first explanation that there may have been a mistake on Ellis Island, and that the four Lithuanian brothers that came over in 1908 were actually Italians.

"Eh...not possible," he would say quite distinctly, as if he had completely forgotten that the truth of who I was dangled so delicately on this information. "Even if they were a hundred percent Italian, your father would not have been a hundred percent, and you would not be fifty percent," he said. "If they were Italian, Jeff and his daughters would also be Italian. I know it shows that Toni's son is your nephew and is Italian, but he has no connection to Ricky. His Italian is not from the same genes as yours." The way he spoke in such a matter-of-fact way, most often with accuracy, was a mix of comforting and downright infuriating.

"The idea that your grandmother fooled around with an Italian and not her Lithuanian husband is also not possible unless your grandmother was also a hundred percent Italian," he noted, and followed up with, "That would mean your sister and brother would have as much Italian as you have, and no one would match Ricky."

So in just a few days, we concluded that those first two scenarios were impossible based on the DNA results. This left only the last scenario: that my mother conceived me with another Italian related to Ricky.

"So now what?" I asked sharply. I was starting to wish we had never opened this box, and I had never mailed off my spit to make my daughter happy.

"Now, you find your father," Billy stated quite simply.

I looked at Kim, my eyes filled with a mix of shock and fear. "Finding my father would also help Ricky find his. I can do this for Ricky."

"No," she kept reminding me, "you can do it for yourself."

Just then, Brad sent me a text: *So you're half of a pizza pie? Does this mean we will have a feast of the seven fishes for Christmas dinner?* He quickly followed it with a video clip of *Family Guy* when Peter goes into an Italian market because he had grown a mustache and begins speaking Italian-sounding gibberish. I laughed, despite the stereotypes. As a defense mechanism, or just because we all have an awkward sense of humor, my kids gravitate towards laughter to lighten the mood, and Brad knew that I had a soft spot for *Family Guy*.

Elton John Concert

It was late February, and Kim had purchased tickets to see Elton
John at our local concert venue with Debbie, Rae Ann, and my
niece Jamie (Rae Ann's daughter). My sisters all loved Elton John
and were exceptionally excited about his concert. They decided
to meet for dinner before the w and carpool to the Times Union
Center in downtown Albany. Kim was running late to the restaurant as usual, so everyone was seated when she arrived.

"Sorry, I'm late! I always get lost around here looking for a parking spot." Kim said, slightly out of breath as she hugged everyone
and got comfortable in her seat at the table.

The waitress circled back, and Kim ordered a glass of wine as she
took her scarf off to hang with her jacket on the back of her chair.

"So! Has anyone spoken to your brother lately?" Kim asked
abruptly. She knew she couldn't sit with my family very long without filling them in on the shocking news we had learned recently,
so there was no sense in waiting to spill the beans.

"Not recently. Is everything alright?" Rae Ann asked, a look of
concern now gracing her face.

The waitress returned with Kim's wine, and she grabbed it
quickly to take a sip. "Boy, does he have something to tell you."

Debbie and Rae Ann looked at each other and then back to Kim, their faces showing a mix of curiosity and worry.

"We really do not know too much right now, but I can tell you that he did his DNA through that Ancestry.com site. Courtney got him a kit for Christmas. Well, it was mainly for Billy. You know, he has always been so intrigued with his heritage and family lineage and stuff." Kim began to turn through the menu, not looking at any of the choices but thumbing it nervously as she shared this news with my sisters.

"So his results came back a few weeks ago," she continued. "And I guess he is fifty percent Italian!" My sisters and niece swapped glances as they awkwardly giggled. They were obviously trying to make sense of what Kim was telling them, but they weren't quite understanding. Kim took another big gulp of her wine, knowing the next shoe she had to drop would not be as funny.

"Which means...your dad was actually not HIS father."

There. She said it. It was like they all froze in time. The table remained awkwardly quiet, despite the hectic sounds of the restaurant that surrounded them. A swirl of chatter, laughter, and the clinking of plates and silverware filled the air as my sisters and niece sat silently, trying to process what Kim had just shared.

"Wait, what do you mean?" Debbie questioned. "I don't understand. What makes you think that?"

"Well, Billy took the test last year and it showed him as twenty-six percent Italian, but we never thought much of it. We had just assumed it was one of those Ellis Island mix-ups, and instead of the Lithuanian brothers, they probably came from Italy. Same stories, just a different boat, right? Billy wanted me to do my DNA to help sort out his. So, of course, Bill did his then, too. And once you do it, the site shows whoever has done their DNA and how they are related to you."

Kim could see that my sisters were still not making sense of the idea that the father who raised me was not my biological father. So, she continued. "As we looked on the site, Chrissy and Debbie, Jeff's daughters did theirs, and they showed up related to Bill as distant nieces, just with zero Italian. This means Jeff has no Italian...but Bill is fifty percent Italian."

This was a lot for my sisters and niece to process. Kim knew this wasn't just a cat but a whole tiger let out of the bag, so she decided to pull back a bit and allow them to stew in everything shared so far. A thick cloud of awkwardness lingered as the waitress returned, and the table ordered their dinner and more wine.

"Well, this is crazy," Jamie exclaimed, breaking the silence. Her mother frowned but remained quiet.

Debbie slumped back in her seat. "Well, I guess that's just another nail in my mother's coffin in Bill's mind," she quipped, referring to the estranged relationship I had with my mother. Kim was beginning to feel uneasy, and wanted to quickly defuse any sense of distress so that the rest of the night was not ruined.

"We don't know much. Bill is doing some digging on the site, but we don't know anything else at this point. I'm sure he will keep you updated once he learns more."

The ladies tried to change the subject and push my news aside to enjoy the evening they had been looking forward to for months.

Elton John's songs played on a loop as their dinners were served, faint in the background. As they ate, the song "Circle of Life" played through the restaurant's speakers and Elton sang of how some of us must live with the scars that come from life's troubles.

Found

After my siblings and I were moved into the children's home, my mother refused to tell any of my family that we were no longer living with the foster family. But we did not know that. So, we sat abandoned in that shelter while my mother gripped onto what was left of her pride. There was no way my mother would willingly confess to my father or Gram that the court took us from her for our safety. Her ego meant more to her than any of us did.

When we first went to the shelter, we barely had any of our belongings, not that we had much to bring anyway. During the first week of October, the days grew colder, so the staff passed out warm clothes and winter jackets. Nothing was new, it was probably donated by the local church, but at least we had something warm to wear. I remember being handed the most fabulous brown bomber jacket I had ever seen. Despite my circumstances, I felt cool as shit in that jacket. It was the best birthday present I ever received (even if it did get me an ass kicking a few months later). I cannot remember if I got the coat on my birthday, October 7th, or if my father arrived to rescue us on October 7th. I want to think it was the latter, and that my father's birthday gift was saving us from the unknown.

I remember it being a Saturday because we didn't walk to school. Without warning, we were asked to pack up all our belongings and sent to wait quietly downstairs in the office. Looking back, they probably didn't want to give us an advanced notice in case something went awry. I'm sure there had been too many times when plans fell through, and children were sent back to rooms filled with disappointment and heartbreak. But not us. I'll never forget seeing my father pull up in that station wagon, ready to take us home. I was still soaked with anxiety, but somehow, I knew the past several years of trauma were behind us. This felt different.

The story goes that my Aunt Lois and Uncle Bill were looking for me. They felt like it had been too long since one of our visits and were feeling unsettled. Unable to contact my mother, they located my Aunt Margaret, who told them we were all taken into custody. Aunt Lois then informed Gram of our situation, who was simultaneously searching for us for weeks. Gram told my father, who then fought for full custody of all of us. Knowing what I do now, the child protective services and family court were methodical and couldn't have worked that fast, so I'm confident that my father must have been working on getting custody long before we were placed in that shelter. My guess is that it all began once we were sent to our foster family.

However, I can't imagine the complexity of my father's situation. By this time, my parents had been long separated, and he remarried a woman named Marge. And now, he had to convince his new bride, with six children of her own, that he had to take the five of us full time. But it wouldn't surprise me if Gram had to nudge him along to do what was right for us. It was not a quick and easy process. There were months of court hearings, with Laurie, Debbie, and me being questioned about our family and who we would prefer to live with. I remember being directed into a private room off the main courtroom and being asked many questions by the judge, all leading to whether we should be allowed to remain in my mother's care. I doubt any of our answers showcased her as Mother of the Year; thus, the court finally awarded custody of all five of us to my father. No one knows the entire truth, but somehow, they had a hunch. All these kids needed a family...that's the way we all became the Aperance/Fortier Bunch?

Life in the Junction

We first moved into Marge's house—a modest, four-bedroom home that had seemed small for the eight of them. Now it was barely livable, with ten children, two parents, and their Hungarian grandma Micski, but somehow my father and Marge made it work. Marge was a strong-minded and hardworking mother. The elementary school was just a few blocks from the house. I still remember all of us walking home from school each day, and Marge would make us soup and sandwiches for lunch. It sure beat old peaches from a Ball jar.

Her oldest son, Ronnie, was from a previous marriage and spent much of his time in the coast guard. When Marge and her family came into our lives, he was away, so we never really lived with him. But how proud they were when he returned from the service and bought the first Ford Mustang to roll off the car carrier in Schenectady. He ended up working for Ma Bell, the New York Telephone Company, where he met his wife Marty, and they are still married today after more than fifty years. Marge's second marriage was to a firefighter, and they had five more children: Joey, Jo-Anne, Peggy, Donna, and Jake. The second husband passed away young, leaving Marge a young widow, on her own with six children. When my father originally came into the picture, he was recently separated, and my siblings and I were still living with our mother. I am sure their life was much simpler. When she fell in love with him, the farthest thing from her mind was that they would soon be taking custody of his brood, too. Now, she had to cook and clean for ten kids and stretch the family income for five more kids she had never signed on for.

As part of the custody arrangements, they immediately had to search for a large "fixer-upper" and found the perfect house in Rotterdam Junction. The Junction was a quiet little village with one gas station, a grocery store, a post office, a bowling alley, a drive-in movie theater, an elementary school, and at least four bars.

My father purchased an old railroad boarding house at the east end of town, big enough for us ten kids and one Hungarian grandmother. Each bedroom upstairs had a number on the door, a bed, a dresser, and a small desk. In its heyday, the Junction was a very strategic railroad switching yard where trains would constantly come and go, so workers would need a place within walking distance for a night or two. What kid wouldn't want to move into a hotel with a number on each bedroom door, even if it was old and run down?

It was a true Brady Bunch situation. Marge's second oldest, Joey, was the same age as my oldest sister Laurie. Both would be out with the local older teenagers later at night doing what teenagers do, and I never got too involved in their activities. In the center of Junction was a Veterans of Foreign Wars hall, a good-sized building with a large wooden floor, perfect for dancing, where they would have music nights with local "up and coming" groups that made feeble attempts to sound like the rock bands of the time. This was just about the time of Woodstock, with several of the more rebellious "hippie types" making the short trek downstate to be a part of the amazing three-day concert. Some say that Joey never really came back from Woodstock. Physically, of course, he did. However, emotionally and mentally, he remained that Woodstock concertgoer—from his long curly blondish hair to his wallet chain and deep love for rock music and motorcycles.

Jo-Anne was Marge's oldest girl and about a year older than me. We got along well. She was charming, and I'll admit, at my age, I had a bit of a teenage crush on her. She was cool, smart, and did well in school. When I got to high school, I found myself wanting to hang out with her whenever I was not occupied with sports. She often took me skiing and never objected to me joining the drama club and being in several musicals with her. Rae Ann and Peggy were in the same grade, and Jeff was the same age as Marge's youngest two twins, Donna and Jake. We were all enrolled in schools within the Schalmont District, and I entered Woestina Elementary to finish sixth grade.

My father was very handy with carpentry and quickly remodeled all the rooms with new paneling and tiled ceilings. Jeff and I got one of the downstairs bedrooms, complete with bunk beds, built by my father. Grandma Micski had a small bedroom right off the kitchen. The house was busy, and with fourteen mouths to feed, we ate in shifts, the younger ones going first. My father built a long dining table in the family room for the kids, with

Dad, Marge, and Grandma Micski eating at the small table in the kitchen. Marge had to stretch her food budget, so she cooked lots of inexpensive Hungarian stews, soups, stuffed cabbage, galump-kis, and "slumgullion" or goulash.

When we first went with Marge and my father, Jeffery, being the youngest, had the most challenging time with the transition, and missed his mother terribly. He was too young to understand that our situation was better than before, and he just wanted his mother. We began weekly visitations to my mother's on weekends, and he would cry and not want to go back. This caused tension between him and Marge, who became frustrated with dealing with this child who didn't appreciate what she was doing for him. Marge thought he needed tough love and discipline to stop his cry-ing, which only exacerbated the situation. Shockingly, my mother took my father back to court. Everyone was baffled when the court awarded her custody of Jeff. This meant that we only now saw him during our sporadic Saturday visitations. Randomly, we would be picked up on a Saturday to spend time with our mother and baby brother.

After separating from my father, my mother couldn't hold a steady income and did whatever she could for money. This meant taking to auction all the tangible, material assets she inherited from the Jefferses. She had an estate sale with everything the Jefferses owned. The mahogany china cabinets, the long dining room table with the formal chairs, the grandfather clock at the base of the stairs, every piece of jewelry of Grandma Jeffers, the fox, rabbit, and mink stoles, the full-length mirrors in the bedrooms, the four-poster beds, every tool from Grandpa Jeffers's shed, and even that 1956 Cadillac convertible. Everything the Jefferses worked for their entire life was apathetically sent out the door in exchange for cash. It became obvious to me that some people are so poor, all they have is money. My mother then dated a man named Al, who helped spend her inheritance. They converted the sunroom at the Big House into a small grocery store for the town. She added on additional apartments and even put in a large, in-ground swimming pool, which was rare in those days.

Unsurprisingly, she was not interested in seeing us during our visitation. I do not recall ever doing anything and only swam in the pool once or twice. She would spend much of the day doing laundry and cleaning the house for those who rented rooms. She may have started working and had to accomplish these chores on our visitation days. Laurie and I were a bit older, had friends and outside activities, and soon found excuses not to go see her.

My siblings and I remember Marge differently, from the "wicked stepmother" to a tough disciplinarian that—maybe not always, but for the most part—treated us five uneducated, under-disciplined, structure-craving kids pretty well. That's the way I saw it. My sisters felt she was a "wicked witch" that treated them with disdain. I understood, as they were younger, and it was probably more traumatic for them to live with someone who obviously did not want or love them. On the other hand, I somehow realized no one could blame her. She was a good-looking, single mother of six kids, recently widowed, who fell in love with my father, a strikingly handsome man who was also recently divorced, with five children.

I can't put myself into any of my siblings' shoes, as each of us had different interactions with our parents.

So, there I was in another new school—my eighth elementary class in six different schools, now in sixth grade—knowing no one, and wearing my prized brown leather bomber jacket. The other boys thought I was a tough guy, looking like James Dean, and decided to take me down a peg or two. Johnny Indian held the current "tough guy" title, so he felt he had to take me on, and kicked my butt. When I got home, Marge discovered the rip in the crotch of my pants. "What the hell happened? Who did this to you?" she asked, in a furious tone. I told her what happened, and she immediately put me in her car and drove directly to Johnny's house, demanding the cost of the pants from his parents. That always stuck with me; she was so mad yet immediately came to my defense, even if she was angrier over having to buy me another pair of pants than me getting the worst of the fight. We had our differences, and she was not shy about dishing out punishment my way, but this time I felt acknowledged and protected.

Marge was a strong-willed Catholic who insisted we attend the local St. Margaret's church. This meant we all had to be re-baptized and confirmed as Catholics. My father and Marge were not allowed to attend service since they were divorced, but they ensured we attended catechism and mass weekly. Although money was extremely tight, Marge was adamant about giving us all an envelope with fifty cents or a dollar to drop in the collection baskets.

I wasn't used to having close friends. I switched schools so much that I was never able to get attached to anyone; frankly, who would want to be our friends anyway? Yet that changed when we entered Woestina Elementary. I became fast friends with Nick Isabella, who also went to St. Margaret's church, and we became altar boys together. Every boy in town was also in the Boy Scouts, which met upstairs in an abandoned building each week. Nicky and I were inseparable, and I would spend a great deal of time at his house.

His mother was small, barely a hundred pounds, with reddish-gray hair, freckles, and a crooked nose. I distinctly remember her: she was very kind to me, and with the chaos at my house, it was a refuge. She was sweet, calm, and involved in every aspect of Nicky's life. She was the epitome of a mother and would always watch over us.

If we were not in school, doing chores, or grounded, we all seemed to find places to go and friends to see. There's one summer day I'll never forget. School was out, and the neighborhood was flooded with kids playing in their yards and riding bikes through the streets. No one could have ever imagined what would happen that day...

There were five of us riding our bikes around town when someone suggested we go get ice cream at the A&W on the other side of the bridge over the Mohawk River. It was one of the original A&W drive-in restaurants, which served those famous frosty glass mugs with A&W root beer, and waitresses would come out to take your order and bring your food to your car. We rode on the steel grating that stretched the length of the bridge and up the hill onto Amsterdam Road, a very busy four-lane highway with a concrete divider separating the oncoming traffic. We followed each other up onto the divider before looking behind us to check that crossing the highway was safe. Then, without warning, I heard the screech of brakes slamming and car tires, followed by metal hitting metal. I stopped as fast as I could, whipping around to see our young friend, Ricky White, rolling up the hood of a car to the windshield and then back down, until he landed face down on the road. I still don't know how it happened.

We were all on the road's right side, going with traffic, but Ricky was behind us. I don't think we realized at the time that he didn't cross over when we all did. He must not have looked back to check if cars were coming. We were all frozen. We couldn't speak, couldn't move. Some kids up ahead sped off to find help, but a few of us just stood there.

I couldn't say how long it took before the emergency vehicles arrived, but it sure felt like time stood still. I stayed on the edge of the scene—I couldn't go any closer, but weirdly, I did not retreat either. The driver of the car and several other bystanders had stopped to help the best they could until the professionals arrived. Then, discreetly, they loaded Ricky onto that ambulance, eerily driving away without any sirens.

His father arrived just as the ambulance pulled away and just stood there with his hands covering his face, trembling, too afraid to take his hands away. He couldn't bear to look down at the pile of twisted metal that hardly resembled a bicycle, a single sneaker caught in the spokes. I just stared at Ricky's father and waited until he eventually looked up and in my direction. His face was as twisted in pain as the bike was. I knew he was already thinking the worst. I don't recall how Mr. White arrived on the scene so fast. He lived just on the Junction side of the bridge. As I remember, during that time, everyone in the Junction had police and fire scanners on in their homes. It is quite possible he heard the call as a volunteer firefighter and knew it was his son.

Our young friend was pronounced dead at the scene. For the next several days, I withdrew to my room, the horrific images from that day replaying in my head over and over again like a movie I couldn't pause. I was unable to shut it off: the look on Mr. White's face when he arrived and saw his son's twisted bike with one sneaker still stuck in the spokes of the wheel and the other several yards away, the way Ricky looked at me as if he knew his fate, but couldn't speak to say goodbye. These moments are forever etched into my memory. It was over fifty-five years ago, yet is as vivid as if it happened yesterday.

This also means over five decades of being haunted by questions I can't answer. We were all between the ages of twelve and fourteen and must have been told by our parents never to cross the Lock 9 bridge. So, whose idea was it? Was it my idea to go, since I had never been there and wanted the damn ice cream? I was still the "new kid," so this was my first time crossing that bridge. Other than with the police that day, I don't remember speaking to anyone directly about the incident, not even to any of the kids who were there. I'll never forget my father and Marge coming into my bedroom and telling me there would be no punishment, as being there and witnessing this horrific accident and losing a friend was punishment enough. They had no idea how correct they were. Maybe I'm the only one out of the five of us who has spent his entire life carrying the guilt from that day. Who knows, but Marge was right about being punished enough, as I've paid dearly for going, whether it was my idea or not.

Maybe it was a coincidence, but I was scheduled to perform the service as an altar boy that warm Saturday morning. I'm not sure why or how it could have been that I was made to perform the funeral service for Ricky, but I would have been too afraid to ask to sit out, since I was involved in the accident. I just showed up terrified and silently performed my tasks. However, I couldn't help but wonder if Father Charles knew I was with Ricky that day and wanted to help me somehow deal with the tragedy. Perhaps he saw that I was struggling with Ricky's death and thought it would be a way of healing or even comforting his parents. My stomach was in knots, and I struggled to breathe in the vestry, helping Father Charles with his dressing following the order of vestments. My palms were sweating as I assisted with the four layers, starting with an amice, then an alb, a stole, and finally a lightweight chasable. For funerals and weddings, the liturgical colors were always white.

The entire village of Rotterdam Junction was there to comfort the White family, who sat just feet away from me as I knelt on the altar. Her face was not visible through the black veil, but Mrs. White's anguish and sobbing was all everyone could hear. Before the service was over, they had to physically carry her out of the church. A thick, dark cloud of sorrow surrounded that family, heavier than I could have ever imagined. I knew everyone was there to pay their respects to Ricky and his family, but I couldn't help but feel their eyes on me, piercing through the darkness, knowing I was one of the boys involved. I did everything possible to avoid looking directly at anyone in the congregation. My heart raced, and I could hardly breathe, but I kept my head down long enough to finish my responsibilities and went home.

Digging Deeper

I realized I had to go deeper into the Ancestry site to locate anyone with the slightest DNA connection to me and go from there. Meanwhile my anger towards my mother for keeping this life-altering secret grew. I was not surprised in the least; however, that didn't make it easier to accept. I began thinking that it was my fault. Maybe if I had maintained a closer relationship with her, she might have opened up, especially after my father passed. Mind you, my mother wasn't known for thinking about others; I doubt she would have volunteered this secret.

It was clear that my mother had an affair with Ricky's father, whoever he was. She had been fooling around with this Italian guy, who then made his way out to Indiana while, at the same time, she still had sex with my father.

One match that came up was a man named Mike Lapinski. Mike came up as a distant second cousin, along with Mary Mulligan and a few others. I was able to cross-check my matches with Ricky's, and they all showed up on his site. I immediately reached out to all of them. Someone had to know something. We were not surprised that we did not get an immediate reply, as many people don't return to the site very often, if at all. Most people complete the

DNA test, check out where they were born and their heritage, and trace it back to their parents and grandparents, but if they do not see any irregularities, they rarely return to the site. My son was one of those who just checked out his nationality and never thought to look any further. Otherwise, he would have seen the message from Ricky months earlier.

At this point, my shock and denial continued to sit heavy in my stomach, yet I went to work to attempt to distract myself. Keeping busy at work has always been my coping mechanism. "And you thought you were the only Italian guy around here!" I joked with Michael Dorato, our Italian sous chef. Dorato took pride in his heritage and loved to tell stories about his family and Italian traditions. Everyone viewed him as the "resident Italian," but now, after this news, he might have to share the throne.

Leave it to Kim to find the irony in me discovering my Italian heritage after spending the last thirty-five years complaining about the local Italian restaurants still serving the same chicken, veal, and pasta dishes from the sixties. Since I had graduated from the world-renowned Culinary Institute of America, I was trained in classical cooking, and "Schenectady Italian" dishes were outside my repertoire. Instead, I cooked with classical French, German, Italian, and Asian influences.

After weeks of obsessively checking the DNA site and spinning my wheels in what seemed like a mud pit of whodunnit scenarios, I finally received a response from Mike Lapinski. Without hesitation, I replied, explaining my situation and informing him that he and I were distant cousins, according to the test results.

Can you tell me the names of your parents and grandparents? I asked in a follow-up text. He gave me several of his grandparents' names, including Carvini, Cassaro, and Caruso. He also noted that they were all local families from the Gloversville– area.

"Have you ever heard of Ernest Conti from Amsterdam?" We hit a wall. I thanked him for his help, even though I wasn't sure it was any help. But it was a start.

We immediately thought that any of these Italian families could have been friends with Ernest Conti, since they were all from the same area. So, I began entering each of these names into the Whitepages website, in hopes of speaking to someone who may have heard of Mike Lapinski, Mary Mulligan, or even my parents.

I was looking for that proverbial needle in a haystack.

Before long, I tracked down a phone number for Mrs. Cassaro from Johnstown. I reached out to her instantly, hoping she could shed some light on how I was connected to these folks who appeared as cousins. My heart raced as I dialed her number. *What will I say?* She answered before I had time to prepare my questions. But there wasn't too much to ask.

"Mrs. Cassaro?" I said. "My name is William Aperance, and I live nearby in Schenectady. DNA testing showed that I was related to Mike Lapinski. He gave Cassaro as one of his grandparents' last names. This would make him and me distant cousins." After I explained what I'd learned about my father, I could tell she genuinely wanted to help me.

Her voice was sweet and kind. "I'm sorry dear," she said sadly, "I do not know anyone by the name of Lapinski." I could hear the disappointment in her tone, as she wished she had more information to provide me.

Before we hung up, I threw a "last-minute pass" out of desperation and asked one more question: "What about Mary Mulligan?" To my surprise and hers, she said proudly, "Oh, she's, my goddaughter!"

Now we were getting somewhere. Excitement mixed with anxiety rushed through my body. She explained that Mary Mulligan's maiden name was Caruso, and she married into the Mulligan family. Mary was listed on my Ancestry website as a distant cousin but had not returned to the site since I posted a message to her.

Mrs. Cassaro continued, "Mary Mulligan's mother, Nancy, and I were very close, but she passed away young, and I have not been in contact with the Caruso family for many years. I believe, but not positively, that one of Nancy's three brothers still lives in Johnstown."

My heart was racing, and I could feel my cheeks reddening. In just those few short moments, she answered many questions; most importantly, that I was somehow related to the Caruso family, and not Cassaro.

She continued. "Anthony...Anthony Caruso," she said. "They called him Duke."

I thanked her for her help and began scouring the internet for anyone by the name of Anthony Caruso, but found only obituaries of his sister Nancy and a younger brother Joey, both of whom passed young. When I was born in 1954, my mother was only twenty-three. So, it made total sense. Anthony, their older brother, was my biological father. Mystery solved.

Mary (Caruso) Mulligan would only share a DNA connection with me if one of her uncles were my biological father. Mrs. Cassaro said there were three brothers, but she wasn't sure how many were still in the area or even alive. I stared at the computer screen, at the name Anthony Caruso. My brain and heart wouldn't allow me to accept this as the final answer. Was this man my father? Was one of his brothers my father? If this man was in his nineties, how old were his brothers? How old were they in 1954? Were any of them even alive? Or was this all another lost cause? I stared at his phone number, which I had jotted on a Post-it, repeatedly flicking the corner edge. I felt a wave of anxiety consuming my entire body just thinking of making this call.

"Do you even want to make this call?" Kim asked matter-of-factly.

"Maybe we should just let sleeping dogs lie. I don't want to give this man a heart attack or stroke," I said as I crumpled up the Post-it and tossed it onto my desk. I got up and went to lie on the couch, assuming my regular position with Sadie at my feet. She had no sense of personal space, but in hindsight, I think she could tell when I needed extra emotional support. I closed my eyes tight, as if closing my eyes meant I could magically close this Pandora's box. I began second-guessing everything. Was discovering who my mother had an affair with worth disrupting someone else's life?

"Even if I make this call, what would make him not think I was some crackpot trying to scam him for his family's money? So he'll just hang up on me."

"Or, he might believe you," Kim stated.

"Yeah, but even if he does, he still may not want anything to do with me," I responded with a snarky tone. I flipped over, now facing the back of the couch, arms still crossed tightly across my chest.

Kim and I had talked about the horrific DNA stories we'd all heard of family secrets that tear apart lives, families, and relationships. It is estimated that there are two million people who have discovered the gut-wrenching truth that they have NPE (Not Parent Expected) since the emergence of genetic testing. On top of that, on average, the news can affect up to fifty other family members, relatives, and friends. I worried about how my sisters and brother would react to us not having the same father. Especially Debbie. She could be sensitive like me and take things to heart.

"You have every right to call and ask, and who knows, maybe it wasn't even him, and it was one of his younger brothers," Kim said. She stood up and went to retrieve the crumpled Post-it from my desk. She pulled it open, smoothed the wrinkles, and placed it on our coffee table beside my cell phone.

"Call him."

In her memoir *Inheritance,* Dani Shapiro asks us, when are we too old to raise the question? It seemed I knew the answer already. You're never too old to question the truth.

Gut Punch

I started to feel like I was stuck on the teacup ride at Disney World. You know the feeling, spinning and swirling about with no control over the direction. Your stomach flips with each teacup that turns towards you and quickly pulls away. I couldn't help but wonder who this man was and if he truly was my father. Yet as my world continued to spin, and I was given each new seed of information leading to the truth, heartbreak set in. I realized it didn't matter who he was; he wasn't MY father, the man who did everything he could to make sure we kids were safe and cared for. The man who spent weeks searching for us despite my mother never confessing that we were taken into custody. The man who everyone said I resembled, with thick, bushy eyebrows and skin that tanned so easily. The man who I idolized so much that I attempted to play baseball like him in Little League, spent way too much money on a drum set (only to learn that I had zero rhythm and coordination), and filled my basement with HO scale model trains, just like his, to share an interest in one of his favorite hobbies. Even after he passed, I purchased his trains from his wife so I would always have something of his. And now, this man I admired, even with all his flaws, wasn't even related to me. This didn't make any sense.

But then it hit me. It wasn't just that my mother was secretly unfaithful, that my father who raised me was, in fact, not my father, or that my siblings had now become only half brothers and sisters; it was Gram. The one person who was always there for us children was in no way related to me. Nothing. Not a drop of common DNA. This was the hardest to accept because Gram was my rock. Truthfully, she was the one person that every one of my siblings adored unconditionally, and never had a harsh word to say about her. How could we? She was incredible. She made sure we had somewhat of a normal childhood.

I'll never forget how she took all of us to a Halloween costume party at the firehouse when I was four. She dressed me in one of her blonde wigs, a dress from my sister, and red lipstick. Everyone thought I was so cute until they found out I was a boy, and then they all had a good laugh, and I won first prize for best costume. In the late fifties and early sixties, she took us all to the big Christmas parade in downtown Schenectady. It was quite the event when General Electric employed over fifty thousand employees who were all there with their families, celebrating the holiday season. Gram would score us the best spot in front of the furniture store so we could wave to Santa and the firetruck floats. To this day, my sister still takes her children and grandchildren to that parade.

Gram was there when we were scared of what was going on with our parents fighting and battling constantly. When we had chickenpox, measles, or the common cold, we went to stay with her. Her place became our safe haven for a night, a week, or months. Frankly, I think we all moved in at some point; Laurie first, then myself, and then the others. As I look back on my life with my father and Gram, it's hard to think that either of them, or anyone for that matter, had any clue that I was not biologically theirs. I can only imagine the pressure and commitment my mother felt keeping that secret from everyone, every day for the last sixty-five years.

The Phone Call

It was the hardest phone call I would ever have to make. After agonizing about it for days, I still wasn't sure I should be making it at all. I had left a simple voice message the day before, hoping I didn't sound like a scammer or some crazy person who'd chosen a random stranger to menace. I realized that this last possibility wasn't so far from the truth.

"I have to call him again," I told Kim. "He might not have listened to the message yet. I'm going outside."

I grabbed my jacket and went out the garage door, letting it slam behind me. I leaned on the trunk of my car, lit a cigar, and tried to take deep breaths, hoping to calm the fuck down. Over the past several days, I had felt a bit insane, and this person whose number I was about to dial was, at this point, still indeed a stranger.

To think that up until a few weeks earlier, everything in my life had felt calm, fulfilling, and predictable. I'd lived a good, hard-working adult life with little turmoil compared to my childhood. My most significant accomplishments included graduating from a prestigious college—after a not-so-prestigious career in high school and an even less impressive stint in the military—being still happily married after thirty-five years, and raising three wonderful children. This is not to say that my career and personal life were without any struggles, but all the ups and downs, successes and failures, and emotional highs and lows were mine and mine alone. The trials and tribulations of my adult life paled in comparison to my childhood.

Still leaning on the back of my car, I finally got up the nerve to make the call. It had been a nice, sunny day, but now the sun went behind the clouds, and the wind picked up. I couldn't tell if I was shivering from the chill in the air or from the nervousness I'd felt all day about the phone call. Probably both. My hands trembled as I dialed his number, making the phone hard to hold. The ring felt like it was two minutes long. Then, I heard a man's voice answer on the other end. Ironically, I felt slightly more at ease when I heard his tender, kind voice on the phone answer pleasantly, "Hello?"

"Hello, Mr. Caruso? My name is William Aperance, and I live in Schenectady." The words instantly shot out of my mouth, like water rushing past a broken dam. I sputtered in fear he would hang up before I finished the sentence.

"I've taken a DNA test and discovered that Mary Mulligan and I are related." Before he could say anything, I continued like my mouth was a volcano and shot out a statement that I never thought I would say: "I believe that you or one of your brothers...could be my biological father."

There was a pause on the other end of the line. The silence was deafening. It may have lasted ten seconds, but it felt like an hour for me. Was he as baffled as I was, perhaps running scenarios in his head and thinking which brother it was? Or worse, was this the moment in which he hung up the phone and my only hope of finding out my truth would be gone? Finally, he spoke.

"Where were you born again?" he asked quietly.

I exhaled with a sigh of relief that he had not hung up. However, the rapid speed in which I spoke did not change, fearing he still could at any moment.

"My mother was Ann Jeffers," I said, waiting for her maiden name to trigger a response. "She lived out on Amsterdam Road outside of Scotia."

There were another few seconds of silence, then he quietly said, "My father had a restaurant on Amsterdam Road." His voice remained soft but intentional. I knew how I felt about all this, so I could only imagine his emotions. I was just glad he was staying on the line.

"When did you say you were born?" he asked.

"October 1954."

He was quiet for a few moments, perhaps calculating my age compared to his.

"What was your mother's name, again? And where did you say she lived?" he asked inquisitively.

"Amsterdam Road, just outside of Scotia, and her maiden name was Ann Jeffers."

We were like two strangers at sea, trying to get our bearings within a dense fog. He told me to call him Duke. I could tell he was no longer thinking it was a prank call, and that now he probably was mulling over which brother it could have been who'd fathered an unknown child. Or what if it was him? What if I was his son?

If he was ninety, he would be my mother's age and the oldest of the sons. Was this the first he was hearing about me? I wouldn't be surprised if he knew about me and wanted nothing to do with me, or better yet, did my mother not let him have any involvement? A wave of anxiety crashed through my body like waves crashing along the shore. I began shaking again as various scenarios spun through my head.

After what seemed like an eternity of questioning each other back and forth, it was safe to say that Duke was burning with curiosity alongside me. Since I was the only one who knew that Ricky had also shown up as my half brother, it was time to ask him the million-dollar question. The question that could indeed narrow down who my biological father was.

"Have you or any of your brothers ever spent time in Evansville, Indiana?"

I felt a rush of anticipation as the words left my mouth, like I opened the floodgates with no chance of closing them. This elicited a long pause, before Duke softly, and somewhat sadly, acknowledged the truth.

"My father did."

Entrepreneurial Drive

For as long as I can remember, I have always had a business venture or job keeping me busy. There was a family who lived down the street from us in the Junction. The older son had a paper route, and his mother wanted to avoid his little brother taking over. Back then, you only had to be thirteen to have a route. Could you imagine parents nowadays letting their thirteen-year-old child walk the street at four in the morning? And then to head back out once a week, typically after supper, to collect payment? Times were different. After hearing that this route might become available, I begged them to give it to me permanently. I had occasionally filled in for the boy, so I knew the map well.

So there I was—a fourteen-year-old businessman responsible for always showing up and being on time, making sure the papers stayed as dry as possible, and most importantly, paying the Schenectady Gazette for the papers they dropped every morning, usually by three a.m. I loved being the only one awake and out on the streets at that hour, especially in the winter. I still recall those times when it snowed overnight. The only sound I could hear was the crunch of my boots as I walked over the freshly fallen snow. The deep silence gave me plenty of time to be with my thoughts.

Occasionally, I'd hear the muffled sound of a dog barking or a car passing. But at that hour, in a small village, it could be forty-five minutes before another car or truck would roll through.

This business venture was quite the experience. The most important thing I learned during this time was to ensure I was paid. I kept very detailed records of who I collected from and who I couldn't. I would go back the next week and remind them they owed for two weeks, and often, they would pause to make sure I was right or even protest, especially if the weeks added up. I had to learn to be firm, stand my ground, and, in some cases, insist I was correct, and they just lost track of the weeks. We had punch cards, but not everyone used them. They learned to trust me, and my collections were well ahead of what I had to pay for the papers. I can't recall the weekly cost of the papers or what I made per customer, but with about sixty or seventy houses on that route, and the generosity of the people who tipped me, I was always flush with money.

Although this was my first official job, it was not my first experience in making and having money. After stealing and returning Pepsi bottles when I was younger, I got a high from having my own money and independence. I still remember how pleased I was to be able to buy my school supplies. Back then, earning money went deeper than just being able to buy my own things. Making my own money showed me that I was worth something despite being raised without much of anything. It showed me that I could have a purpose and a place in society. Watching how my mother handled jobs and money (or lack thereof) played a huge role in the fact that I would spend the rest of my life trying to feel successful through my work. Did it become an obsession? Perhaps. The fact that I always had money made me want to work more.

For a while, I helped clean the bar my father had opened in the middle of town, right about where my paper route ended. Each morning, once I finished my route, I would head into the bar to do a quick cleanup from the night before. This consisted of sweeping and mopping the floors, sorting empty beer bottles, and taking out the trash, not before dumping all the ashtrays that were purposely left on the bar to be sure they wouldn't start a fire overnight. I then would catch the bus to school around seven a.m. None of this was forced labor or any punishment. Since I was already awake, I'm sure I offered to help so he would be proud of me and my work ethic. Like my father, I wanted to be seen as a hard worker, and I wanted to eliminate the need for anyone to support me fully.

I also remember helping the butcher in the meat section of the small local grocery store. I would clean the knives, sweep and mop the floor that got so greasy it seemed like you were skating around on your sneakers, and use a brush made of steel metal strips to scrub the meat and fat built up on the wooden butcher top tables. I would help with stocking the counters and even had to dismantle and clean the band saw, one of the most dangerous pieces of equipment. I can't recall any rules regarding child labor laws or any regulations with local health departments. And even if there were, no one seemed concerned. The butcher, Joseph Pugliano, was a first-Italian American. He taught me all the swear words in English and Italian and loved showing off his early 8 mm porn collection from the fifties. They were black and white and very grainy, but man, was he proud of those films.

This was a very stable time in my life with a few good friends and steady jobs. I would start each day around four a.m., and Jeff and I had bedrooms downstairs so I could sneak out of the house and not worry about waking anyone else. Life finally felt "normal," or at least my version of normal. Eventually, I gave up the paper route and only worked part-time at the grocery store, stocking shelves. As I entered high school, I wanted more time to play sports, hang out with friends, and get involved in other activities.

Once I turned seventeen, I felt it was time to leave the packed house with all my siblings, and I went to live with Gram. By this time, the drunken, abusive predator Ray had drunk himself to death, so I knew she could use the company in the house. Being a year older than my friends, I was the first to get my license and a car. This allowed me to drive to school daily and get a dishwasher job at a local restaurant. The Turf Tavern was a family-owned business operated by Steve and Fanny Karamanos. At first, I was stationed at the back pot sinks where the cooks would toss the hot pots and sizzle platters into the sink from ten feet away, making it splash up in my face, giving all the cooks a good laugh. Yet, Steve quickly noticed my work ethic and promoted me from dishwasher to pantry cook, preparing all the appetizers, salads, and desserts.

Nick and I watched the summer of '73 wind down and realized we had no future if we stayed in the Junction. Both of our families didn't have much, so college was never an option for us. This was during the post-Vietnam era when pretty much anyone who wasn't headed off to college to become a doctor or a lawyer ended up enlisting in the military. At first, we decided to take the air force exam, mainly because Nick's older sister had enrolled a few years prior, and it was familiar to us. I scored high in electrical engineering, so they planned to send me to Colorado for electrical engineering school. I recall Nick succeeding in mechanical engineering, as he was pretty handy and always fixing things, just like his father. Ultimately, none of this mattered because, at the time, we realized it made more sense for us to enlist in the army. My dream was to become a New York state trooper, so I thought entering the army to become a military police officer made the most sense.

Ironically, Nicky and I were dating sisters Barb and Beth Rumney from Scotia. Barb was my first real girlfriend, and we spent a lot of time together. She was younger so it was just puppy love and we said goodbye and promised to keep in touch.

Basic training went exactly how it has been portrayed in movies: drill sergeants screaming, grown men in tears, some so terrified they tried to sneak out in the middle of the night and go AWOL. Ironically, I almost felt prepared for it. Being lined up and yelled at was nothing new to me. Basic was more challenging than I imagined, but my mother (with all the qualities of a drill sergeant) had already prepared me for the worst. The bonus was that we were never beaten or whipped in basic.

Nick and I were at Fort Dix simultaneously with my cousin, Bobby Rice. On the day of our training graduation, I recall Aunt Audrey and Nick's mom and siblings coming down to celebrate.

I don't remember anyone from my family making the four-hour trip, but in their defense, I doubt I invited them. After basic, we had a week or two home on leave before receiving orders of where and when to report to our respective Advanced Individual Training (AIT). This was when Nick and I headed our separate ways.

I was headed off to Fort Gordon, Georgia, as part of the 556th Military Police Company. After eight weeks of military police training, I learned I would be stationed at a US military base in Siegelsbach just outside Heilbronn, Germany. Siegelsbach was used for storing munitions, and it was the 556th Military Police officer's job to guard and protect this "high security" base rumored to house Trident missile warheads during the Cold War.

When we arrived that first night, we were immediately halted by the MP on duty at the front gate. After glancing at our vehicle, he lifted the large bar gate, and we drove through. I was in awe as we went towards the main road to get to the two-story barracks reserved for the MPs. We passed the barracks for the munitions and mechanic companies, motor pool, dog kennels, mess hall, post exchange, and movie theater. It all seemed glamorous to us, especially when we were fortunate enough to be assigned to "white hat" duty, which was our chance to head off base and ride around the streets of Heilbronn like we were real cops.

Okay, maybe not real cops, but we were responsible for breaking up any street fights and getting all the drunk GIs back to their barracks before the German police got involved. In our downtime, we loved driving around, pulling along the curb to flirt with any

German fraulein who walked by. We would shout out the window, "Ich liebe dich, mein Schatz!" (*I love you, my sweetheart*), handing the ladies a flower, making them giggle. Unfortunately, my days patrolling Heilbronn were short-lived. This duty was reserved for those who were exemplary soldiers without write-ups or demotions. I was not one of them. I had no intentions of being a "lifer" and just wanted to have fun and get the GI Bill benefits.

My first summer there, we would work long stretches and then get several days off, so we would travel all over Europe. On a trip through the Black Forest, I bought and shipped a beautiful cuckoo clock back to Barb along with letters professing my love. Her parents did not see us continuing our relationship as she was heading to college, and I soon got the inevitable "dear Bill" letter.

My fellow MPs called me the "company class clown." I was just too immature and tried to make everything funny. But you know what wasn't funny? Within a very short time of my goofy behavior, I rolled a jeep in the security zone and was caught buying Jack Daniels whiskey and Marlboro cigarettes from the post exchange to sell to Germans on the street. I was relegated to tower duty...full-time "tower rat." Never seeing white hat duty again.

The towers were no more than six feet square, forty feet in the air, with room for just a stool and a radio. There was not enough room to stretch out if we wanted to sleep, so we just sat on the stool and leaned back with the front two legs off the ground. The towers were very far apart, so we could see the lights of any oncoming jeep as long as we didn't doze off. But let's be honest, it was the perfect place to doze off. I remember some sergeants or lieutenants would be so determined to catch us sleeping on duty that they would drive down the road between two twenty-foot fences topped with barbed wire. When they got close, they would shut off their lights and slow down, creeping towards the tower so quietly that there was no way we would hear them, especially with the radio on. I was busted more times than I would like to admit, accompanied by a demotion or loss of a stripe. That was the worst disciplinary action because our rank was tied to our pay. Plus, we were assigned shittier duties, and I lost any chance of a "white hat" duty off base. So, for the remainder of my time stationed in the woods of Germany in peacetime, I sat crouched in a tower, listening to Olivia Newton John's newest single, watching small deer and giant rabbits wander by and trying my darndest not to fall asleep.

I had been at Seigelsbach, or "the Bach" for short, for about a year and a half and was in my second summer there when I met Lynn, an American foreign exchange student staying with a German family in Siegelsbach. Within a few weeks, I was in love. I spent most of my days distracted by Lynn. It was one thing to always be on the sergeant's bad side for sneaking Lynn into the barracks at night; sleeping on duty the following day, that was the icing on the cake.

In hindsight, I was never meant to be a soldier. I was so easily distracted by my new love and life off base that once Lynn returned to the States, I became depressed and began acting out. Back home, Marge was diagnosed with cancer. The disease took hold of her throat, lymph nodes, and tongue. Her case was beyond the capabilities of our local hospital, so she was referred to the Roswell

Park hospital in Buffalo. I shamefully used her illness as a reason to get out of the military early. I had less than a year to go, but Lynn had returned to the States several months earlier, and I was anxious to get back to be with her. So, the opportunity presented itself, and I accepted a reasonable, honorable discharge and was granted all my GI Bill benefits except one: I'm not eligible to be buried in Arlington National Cemetery. The military had more than enough recruits at the time and allowed anyone who wanted out to leave if they had a reasonable excuse or a history of warnings and demotions. I had both and was soon sent back to the States, only to find that Lynn had moved on and I was just a summer fling.

My time as military police officer overseas helped solidify the fact that I wanted to become a trooper. After my discharge in 1975, I immediately started the process of joining the police force. I scored well on the trooper exam; however, New York state was financially bankrupt then, and stopped accepting recruits to the trooper training center. With my dreams of entering the police force quickly fading, I moved back in with Gram and returned to the Turf Tavern. The Karamanos family eagerly took me back, this time training me as a line cook. Each day I went in, I did whatever I could to become the best line cook they had seen. I was punctual, professional, and hardworking. I began to enjoy cooking, and truthfully, I was really good at it. My determination didn't go unnoticed. Steve Karamanos came into the kitchen one day and asked if I had ever considered making a career out of cooking. Taken aback, I told him how I had aspired to become a NYS trooper, but the timing was off. Never in my wildest dreams could I imagine myself becoming a professional chef. Alas, after his encouragement, letter of recommendation, and written proof of two thousand hours committed to an existing restaurant, I was accepted into the number one culinary school in the country, and began classes the following fall.

The GI Bill allowed me to attend the Culinary Institute of America in their two-year associate degree program. Here, I was able to hone my craft and become formally trained, learning everything from basic baking to designing wedding cakes with pulled sugar and decorative pastillage, to meat cutting, ballotine, and preparing large charcuteries. It was my first exposure to cooking (and eating) different cuisines, predominantly Asian, German, and French. The quality and quantity of culinary art were beyond anything I could have imagined. However, it was the management and hospitality accounting classes that most interested me. During one semester, I was lucky enough to manage a small hotel south of the school. I spent my days in class, and at around three p.m., I would head directly to the hotel and manage until ten p.m. or later. I knew then that handling the business and operations gave me the most satisfaction. Then I was given an opportunity to leave the hotel and double up on classes to graduate after only eighteen months. With my experience at the Turf Tavern, the Culinary Institute waived the need for further internship so I could graduate.

After finishing college, I ended up bouncing around a few different beach resorts and restaurants, working as head chef. I eventually returned to Schenectady and landed the executive chef position at The Willows Country Club in Rexford for two years.

The Edison Club was a much bigger club and was just down the road from the Willows. Their chef, Pat Rocco, had a heart attack and I was quickly hired to replace him; this is where I met Kim. This was the start of my forty-two-year career in private country clubs as chef, club manager, and finally general manager. After several years, Kim and I were credited with saving The Edison Club from bankruptcy, and with two small children, I was itching to get a better management position and make more money to support my family.

With the help of a Midwest headhunter, we found a beautiful club out west in Lima, Ohio, not too far from where Kim's parents grew up. It was a small club with a membership made up of anyone who was anyone in the town, a delightful mix of "old money" and the "well to do" younger generation. It was a much different and harder job than The Edison Club because the members had much higher expectations. So, as per usual, I put everything I had into managing that club's operations, while keeping under budget. I worked hard and it was appreciated by their board and most of the membership. With Kim's experience as Banquet and Dining Room Manager at The Edison Club, I was able to bring her on board to manage their dining room part-time, as we now had three babies at home to take care of.

What was interesting was the more comfortable I felt in my role as general manager at any club, the more restless I became. I was never satisfied. I was always looking for the "next best thing" or a new opportunity to occupy my time, and just managing the club was never enough. There was a fire in me to work hard to create another opportunity that would support my family and me, while still running the best club operation I could. I suppose this was just my way of working my ass off in hopes that one day, my work would not rely on club members.

For a long time, my entrepreneurial schemes and inventions were just me putzing around to occupy my time and my mind. Like when mobile phones were just becoming popular, so I thought of a delivery service where a customer would call a number (224-FOOD), and order takeout from any one of a dozen locations. The thought was that the customer would pay me a surcharge on the food, and I would get a ten percent discount from all the partnering restaurants. Unfortunately, in 1985, no one understood the vision so the Door Dash concept would have to wait another thirty-five years.

At the same time, the Midwest became the hub of experimental food concepts, and double lane drive-thru restaurants from Carl's Jr, Snapps, and Checkers were popping up everywhere. I was instantly intrigued by this new concept and my entrepreneurial drive kicked in. Anytime I worked on a hobby or idea, it was an attempt to escape my reality and be my own boss. Until that one time when my obsession led me to a particular roll of the dice, which, for the first time, had real consequences.

I discussed my vision with some wealthy club members who I knew had the financial capabilities to back me. I convinced them there would be a worthwhile return on their investment if they helped with land and construction costs. They agreed, and I designed the restaurant from the inside out. We found what we thought was a perfect location, right off the main four-lane commercial highway through the town, next to a Walmart. The process started smoothly, until I came up against an unforeseen development. There were plans to build a bank next to me, and the logistics of having two adjacent construction projects complicated my own plans. I no longer had the ideal circumstances for the restaurant I had envisioned, and costs rose beyond my expectations. But I was in too deep, and my entrepreneurial addiction was far too great for me to stop once my mind was made up. Unfortunately, I became desperate and broke the cardinal rule when starting a business venture: investing more than you can cover, resulting in borrowing money from family. My mother-in-law loaned me a significant amount as a last-ditch effort in saving the restaurant, which of course, added a whole new layer to my unwavering stress. Regrettably, "Manhattan Express" and my dream of a franchise double drive-thru restaurant ended as quickly as it began, leaving me no other choice than to file for bankruptcy.

Before, I had always made sure to invest my time and energy into side projects only once I felt confident in the control I had over my full-time management job. However, this project consumed me and all my effort, so the club's board had no other choice than to let me go.

I'll never forget sitting on the edge of the bed, crying my eyes out, thinking about how selfish and stupid I was. I apologized relentlessly to Kim for leaving us with no savings or income, about to lose the house, with three babies under the age of five. Looking back, I often wonder if my emotions in that moment were solely based on the fears I had for the future of my family, or because I was quickly brought back to a feeling of worthlessness that, through the years, I had worked so hard to overcome. The shame I felt when we filed for bankruptcy was too familiar. I had lived so much of my life feeling inferior to those around me, especially at the clubs I worked at. Now, as my choices affected my wife and children, my business failure and hitting rock bottom extinguished any remnants of self-esteem I had left.

But giving up was not an option for me. We packed up the kids and headed north to the great state of Michigan. I applied to a wonderful country club, north of Detroit in Bloomfield Hills. Ahead of the interview at Forest Lake CC, I drove to the club to see the clubhouse and surrounding areas. This facility was nestled in quite the affluent neighborhood and overlooked the lake. The membership was extremely well-off, which made me more insecure than ever before, especially with what I had just gone through. I knew I had no shot at this job. Why would they hire a guy like me? Coming off the devastating blow of failing at a business venture, losing my previous job and filing for bankruptcy, I had zero self-confidence. Therefore, with nothing more to lose and knowing I had no chance at this job, I drove down the road and turned into what appeared to be the local hangout. It was midafternoon on a Wednesday, and I sat down at the end of the bar and ordered a single malt scotch. Now, I admit, there's nothing more humbling than sitting in a bar in the middle of the workday when you are used to working seventy-plus hours a week. I knew there was no chance that they would hire me for this club, but

I knew I had to at least show up to the interview with nothing to lose. I gathered my thoughts, finished my drink, and made my way to the clubhouse. I am not sure whether it was me losing all hope or the scotch, but somehow during that interview, I found my confidence and convinced the board that they needed a guy like me to manage their club.

When they hired me, one of the biggest selling points for me was that they were going through a multi-million-dollar renovation. For the first year, I was able to help coordinate the finishing of the new clubhouse, hire over a hundred new employees, and open the operation on a dime. This was where I thrived. I was able to set the standards after a new renovation and worked tirelessly to make the necessary changes for the club to become successful. Of course, I hired Kim as my assistant to oversee the food and beverage operations. However, the club's employees were protected and supported by the Teamsters union. It made it almost impossible for me to manage this club how I wanted (and how it needed to be managed) when the union fought every decision I made. Kim, the kids, and I were alone in this new city with no family or friends nearby, and despite the club being just what I needed, the union made it unbearable. I began sending my resume out to clubs all over the northeast, but ultimately, Kim and I knew we wanted to return home to New York.

Luckily, I secured an interview at Colonie Country Club in Voorheesville, NY. I still remember waiting in the lobby of their small, unimpressive facility, that seemingly looked trapped in the sixties. It was a much smaller operation compared to my previous clubs in the Midwest, but it would be fine because we were back home and closer to our family. During this time, Kim began working at a large hotel in downtown Albany, but then was quickly lured to an opportunity at Albany Country Club that she couldn't pass up.

Meanwhile at Colonie, I convinced the membership that their antiquated clubhouse was not going to hold up compared to the other clubs in the area, and once again, I supported and oversaw another multi-million-dollar renovation. The club was thriving after remodeling; however, after seven years, board members changed, as did their vision and expectations. What many people are not privy to is that whenever a club goes through a renovation, with most of the costs falling on the membership, soon after, they feel compelled to change management. Regardless of how smoothly the renovation process may go, the membership has the impression that a new clubhouse means a new manager. That, and *many* other reasons, is why the average lifespan of a general manager at a private club is only about four years. Seeing the writing on the wall, I remained proactive and searched for a new position. As luck would have it, The Edison Club hired me for a second time to help them through their first renovation since the club was built in 1927. This time the club was in much better financial condition and the members were thrilled with the renovation.

Once I felt comfortable in the daily operations at Edison, my entrepreneurial obsession crept back in. Ironically, at the same time, a local valet company that serviced all the local clubs went out of business and the owner left town. This obviously was the perfect business venture for me to take over. I remained fully committed to my management work, but now invested any extra time I had into turning my new business into a successful side project. With every car we parked, we left a Classic Valet business card in the center console, which ultimately helped expand our business dramatically. We became so profitable we were able to purchase limousines to complement the valet services. Finally, I had a place to invest my time and energy that wasn't solely into the lives of country club members. I was my own boss and was able to create a business that made enough money for my family to benefit from. As the operation grew, I was fortunate enough to have my brother-in-law, Larry, as a partner to help manage the clients and bookings. Before long, we expanded the company to include ten limousines, a party bus, and a twenty-passenger Escalade. Luckily for us, we sold the limousine business in 2008, just before the stock market crashed, cashing out before the limo business tanked.

As per usual, after The Edison Club went through their massive renovation, and so much of my time and energy was spent with Classic Valet & Limo, I could sense my time as their manager was running dry. Coincidentally, Albany Country Club was looking for a general manager to work alongside Kim. They already knew how smart and hardworking she was, so they had no reservations hiring me, especially with my strengths in food and beverage operations. So, we worked our fourth club together, increasing business, reducing all costs, remaining overall profitable, and trying our best to keep our membership happy. I luckily continued working side by side with Kim for the next seventeen years.

Johnstown Luncheon

After my phone call with Duke, it was clear that we had solved the puzzle: he and I were half brothers, along with Ricky. But both of us came out of this conversation shaken. From the first phone call until we made the drive up to Johnstown to meet Duke and his family for the first time, there was so much of the past running through my head. I wondered what the future would bring. Who was this man? Who was this family?

A few days before the drive, I reached out to a friend of mine, Ryan, who was very knowledgeable about everyone in that area. "Have you ever heard of a Caruso family?" I asked. Then, clarifying, "Anthony Caruso, maybe about ninety years old?"

"Sure," Ryan responded. "Great guy! My aunt lives in the same apartment complex as he does. He was the deputy mayor after a long career working with a state-run facility for underprivileged boys." A sense of relief settled. Up to now, I did not know much about him other than he was the son of a restaurant owner who most likely was my biological father.

It was a sunny early April morning, and I was extremely anxious even after taking my anti-anxiety medication. As we got on the thruway, I had a cigar to try and remain calm. Kim didn't like me smoking in her car but allowed it, knowing I was a nervous wreck. My one hand clenched the wheel while the other held the cigar close to the window, although the odor had already filled the car. I felt a rush of conflicting emotions. Did I really want to go down this road? What would my siblings think about me meeting Duke, or even worse accepting him as my brother? Especially Debbie, who I feared would feel that this would strain my relationship with my current siblings even further. Or what if Mr. Caruso changed his mind after our phone call and his family rejected me as a half brother?

It was not that long of a drive, but it gave me plenty time to recall the remainder of the phone call with Duke. It was almost hypnotic, the call replaying in my mind as the mile markers whizzed by on the guard rails that separated us from the dark brown, muddy Mohawk River almost the entire drive. My mind recalled every detail of that conversation. But it was his answer to my question that was etched into my memory.

"My father did."

During our call, with information provided by Ricky's search, Duke and I were able to piece together that it was his father, Louis Caruso, who was my father, and not him or his younger brothers. This also answered the question of how Ricky and I were related, since now I knew that Duke's father had spent time in Indiana, fathering another child in 1958.

Even more interesting was that the Jeffers, my mother's adopted parents, actually owned that parcel of land across the street where Duke's father opened his restaurant. Duke remembers having to walk the rent check over to the "old man" across the street. Despite his hatred of Italians after my mother's failed marriage to Conti, begrudgingly, Grandpa Jeffers must have leased it out to Duke's father for a restaurant.

The GPS woke me from my daze as it confirmed we were twenty minutes to our destination. A wave of heat consumed my body, like an anxiety attack. I'd had them all my life, so I took several more puffs of the cigar as we followed the river and watched the mile markers whiz by on my right. The closer we got to Johnstown the more my mind raced as I questioned myself, *what the hell are you doing? Adding a whole new family, when you have avoided the one you already have?*

"Just up here on the right," Kim said, and was finally able to shut off that annoying GPS. We pulled into the parking lot of the Holiday Inn, which was easy to find and probably hadn't changed a bit in several decades.

"We'll just meet them, have a nice lunch, maybe learn a few things about my biological father and this man. That's it," I said firmly, despite the obvious fear that resonated in my voice.

"There is no obligation to go any further than today. Let's just go meet them and take it from there," Kim assured me, jokingly adding, "We'll have a nice lunch and add them to our Christmas card list."

I dropped Kim off at the front entrance and I found a parking spot far away from the hotel, my last-ditch effort to hide from this man and this whole situation. I got every last puff out of that cigar before getting up the nerve to go in. Sitting there in silence,

I finished my cigar and dropped it into the cold, leftover coffee in the cupholder.

Kim later revealed that she had wanted to go in first and had hoped to get a chance to speak to them before I came in. She wanted them to know how disoriented and confused I had been after learning all these revelations.

"Bill's mother would never have won any Parent of the Year awards," she told him.

"Neither would our father," Duke said with a grin.

It felt surreal, like an out of body experience. My anxiety rose as I walked towards the front door. It was noon on a Tuesday in Johnstown and the parking lot was pretty empty so we were sure the place would be quiet. Walking into the darkened entrance of the lobby, I paused to allow my eyes to adjust from the sunlight.

Duke and I had never met in person, nor had I seen any pictures, but after a quick scan of the lobby, our eyes met, and I knew it was him. He was a bit older with a gentle face and a smile that lit up the lobby. He was slightly shorter than I, maybe five-nine, balding slightly and in fantastic shape for his age, which we now knew was not ninety but early eighties, making him seventeen when I was born. Duke eagerly came towards me with such pride, like he was coming up the eighteenth green to drop the winning putt. He immediately gave me the biggest hug and kiss on the cheek. My heart swelled and a rush of unfamiliar emotions filled my body.

We introduced ourselves to his lovely wife Edna, daughter Jeannine, and his niece Mary Mulligan. A tall, slender waiter immediately escorted us to a private table in the dining room. Duke made sure we sat next to each other, with his wife on his left and Kim on my right. Edna was quiet and soft-spoken, with a kind but confident face, the stereotypical sweet Italian grandmother with an honest sincere smile. Jeannine was just as sweet, a retired elementary school teacher, and shared her parents' smiles. She was easy to talk to, and between my wife and her, they kept the conversation moving along. Mary was quiet and seemed a bit uncomfortable, but I'm not sure the families remained too close once Duke's sister passed so young.

We began lunch and got caught up with the initial pleasantries, then we discussed how incredible the story was and how this all came together so quickly.

"We just found out the DNA results on Valentine's Day," Kim said, "and here we are in April. Often, people are searching for years, their whole lives, for their family members, let alone having lunch with them a few months after finding out their truths."

Kim and I gave them a quick description of our marriage, our life together, and shared all about our three grown children.

"You have a wonderful family, and you should be proud of that," Duke reminded me. After only knowing each other for a few minutes, this man spoke to me as if he had known me my whole life. There was such a comfort when speaking to him. He had a way of making every one of my walls, built high with anxiety, fear, and depression, slowly come down. Not crumble dramatically, but rather brick by brick, in the most calming and genuine way.

Our waiter, a young man named Ralph, barely left the perimeter of our table. It was obvious he was intrigued by our situation and hovered so as not to miss any part of this meeting and our story. There was still a small ounce of doubt that lingered in my mind. I kept thinking, *What if you're missing something and this guy isn't who you think?* That was when Duke handed me a large tan envelope, and with pride in his voice he softly said, "Here's a picture of OUR dad."

I was trembling as I cautiously pulled out an eight by eleven glossy picture of our father. Chef Louis Caruso was in full chef whites, wearing a very tall toque which signified a chef's talent. The taller the toque the more he was respected in the field. In addition, he proudly wore the impressive medals he had been awarded for his lifelong achievements in the culinary profession.

"You turned white like you had seen a ghost when you saw that picture," Kim told me afterwards.

There I was. Sitting in a hotel dining room, at the age of sixty-five, seeing a picture of my father for the first time. The others at the table stayed quiet as I stared at the photo, examining every facial feature. The resemblance was undeniable. His nose, eyes, thin lips, and a bit of a lazy eye.

"He was an award-winning chef," Duke said proudly.

I just nodded. I was speechless. As I stared at my father, the others shared information and stories about him. During our initial phone conversation, Duke had indicated that his father had owned that restaurant, but I only assumed he was an unknown, Italian "cook" who bounced around from Gloversville to Schenectady and probably would never have made anything of himself. Now I learn that he was an award-winning, professional, culinarian?

My mind wandered back through the process of putting it all together as everyone chatted. I realized that his restaurant was right across the street from my mother's house, and I imagined him cooking in this small, old kitchen, flirting with every young woman in that place. I have a feeling Duke could tell that this was something I was wondering about and told me that his father had closed the restaurant within months of my birth and moved out west to Indiana. Even though I had never met him, it was obvious he wanted nothing to do with me. I felt a twinge of heartbreak. This was nuts; how could I be sad over someone I never met?

Duke, Edna, and Jeannine filled me in on Chef Lou's life up to that point. He went into the navy as a young man with experience in restaurants; they assigned him to cook on a hospital ship off the coast of Guadalcanal. When he was discharged, it was suggested that he remain in a warmer climate because he had caught malaria, which was common for soldiers in the Pacific. He stayed in California and became the chef manager of a club on the base. He eventually moved his family out from Johnstown to California by train in 1945, when Duke was quite young. He put his family up in housing near his work, however was not home all that much since he worked long hours. His wife soon became unhappy and wanted to return to New York. Chef Louis listened to his wife and returned to this area, where he worked several restaurants, one of which was the well-respected Hotel Van Curler in Schenectady, eventually opening the infamous "Caruso's Little Taste of Italy" restaurant across from my grandparents' house. They went on to tell me that he had worked numerous jobs after he moved out to Indiana but came home several times a year to visit and flash around his money. That was his way of checking in on everyone. "Everyone came to visit when Lou was home!" they told us.

I sat there, dumbfounded. Ralph came back to the table and served our lunches and refilled our waters. Good thing, as my mouth was so dry, it was becoming difficult to speak. I drank my glass so fast Ralph was able to fill it again after circling the table. I started to pick at my lunch, even though at this point of hearing all about my biological father, my appetite had diminished.

The similarities of our lives were striking—almost unbelievable. We both were in the service. We both were at the Culinary Institute (he as a professor, me as a student) and had experiences working in hotels, country clubs, and even opening our own restaurants. We both liked to flash our money around to prove our success, and we both had an entrepreneurial spirit. Duke then shared that he used to help his father at the restaurant on weekends and after school, since he was the oldest of the three brothers at seventeen.

"I have to share with you something that I have never spoken of to anyone, but I remember this moment like it was yesterday," he said as he reached for my hand. "I was working in the restaurant and we received a phone call. The lady on the other end said 'Mr. Caruso?' I knew my father was busy in the back, so I just said 'Yes?' That is when this soft, pleasant voice on the other end said, 'This is the maternity ward at Ellis Hospital calling to let you know that your wife just had a baby boy.'" He recalled not knowing how to respond and quickly handing the phone to his father like a hot potato, saying, "Dad, it's for you!"

"I remember it was so strange since my mother was older and certainly was not pregnant. In fact, it was such a bizarre call that I could never forget it."

"What did your father say?" I asked.

"We never spoke about it," he said as a matter of fact.

"When you called, I began to put the pieces together," he said confidently "It came back to me like it was yesterday." Duke may have been in his early eighties; however, he was sharp and showed no signs of memory loss.

This would have made Louis forty-two at the time, and my mother twenty years younger. The thought of my mother cheating with a chef from the restaurant she worked at was not a shocker, but with that big of an age gap? Furthermore, why did she give the hospital his information as the father? Where was my father? She already was married twice and had three young children at home. Was she hoping he would leave his wife for her?

Throughout the lunch, Duke would reach over, hold my hand, and give me a loving smile, tears welling up in his eyes. I could tell that he was truly happy that we found each other. It was a very strange and unfamiliar feeling that someone that I had just met, even being connected by our DNA, could express such loving emotion towards me. No other adult or family member has ever made me feel like he did during that lunch: honestly, unconditionally loved. If only I had received that more as a child, I thought.

"You have his hands," Duke said softly as he reached over to pat mine.

The more I thought about Louis, the more I felt cheated in some way. The similarities I shared with this man were uncanny, but this secret was kept from me for so long.

"You look more like Dad than any of the other brothers."

It became apparent that Duke's emotions were twofold. Without a doubt, he was beyond thrilled that my search had led me to him. Yet, the more he spoke to me, the more obvious it was that I was a conduit to his relationship with Louis. Seeing me triggered the memories and feelings Duke had of our father, through my physical traits as well as our comparable lives.

As our time at lunch continued, there was no longer any doubt in my mind. Duke watched me intently and saw that I was trying to make sense of these revelations. He leaned closer to me and softly asked, "If you're still unsure, would you like me to take a DNA test?"

I stared at the picture, looked at Kim who was smiling, and then back at Duke. "There's no need, you are my brother!"

Ralph returned to clean up our table. He was smiling ear to ear, and even looked a bit emotional. Working in hospitality for decades, I knew that servers would listen to guest conversations, and he was never out of earshot.

"Would you like me to take your picture of you all?" he offered, realizing that this was an occasion we wanted to remember forever. We all got close and smiled. For the first time in a while my smile was so genuine my cheeks were starting to hurt.

We ended our lunch and Ralph brought over the check. I made sure that I picked up and as I was signing it, Duke chuckled. With a sheepish grin, he leaned in and said, "Just like your father...always flashing his money around and picking up the tab when he was home visiting."

We kept holding hands and would stop only long enough to wrap our arms around each other's shoulders or for me to hug and say goodbye to Edna, Jeannine, and Mary. As we approached the hotel exit, Duke looked into my eyes and leaned in. He squeezed me tight, the type of hug that told me with every part of his being, that he was there for me. At that moment, I felt like the luckiest man in the world. In a weird way, I felt complete.

The Ride Home

"Well, that was lovely! I'm guessing this will be more than just sending a Christmas card?" Kim said with a smirk as she buckled her seatbelt. I couldn't help but smile back, partly because I was happy but partly because I was still in shock over what had just happened. I pulled out of the hotel parking lot to head home. The ride gave me time to reflect on everything thrown at me during that lunch. I had no reference points on how to process meeting family members you never knew existed, let alone finding out a ton of information about your secret biological father. As I lit another cigar, I instantly became overwhelmed. *I was thrust into these people's lives, and now I feel determined to know more about them—their past, their families, everything.*

"They all said that of all the brothers, you looked the most like him," Kim reminded me as she slid his photo back out. "I think it's the eyes."

I glanced over to his picture on the manila envelope on her lap and then back on the road ahead. "Yeah, I guess I do resemble him."

But the resemblance went deeper than just physical. Glancing at that picture again, I couldn't help but still feel shocked to know that he, too, was a chef. But not just any chef in any old restaurant.

He was a true professional, his chef coat decorated with all his culinary medals. Since finding out that Chef Lou was indeed my father, I struggled with having any ounce of respect for him as a father who could sacrifice his family for his career. I felt so torn. I took another puff of my cigar and blew it out the window. This man knew about me but wanted nothing to do with me, yet I have always respected any professional chef who chose and committed themselves to that career.

And it didn't help to learn that he spent time as a chef instructor at the Culinary Institute in New Haven, Connecticut. I could envision him walking the halls of that prestigious school, with his crisp, white chef coat and his tall, white toque, nodding to all the students who would pass him saying, "Good Morning, Chef!" Duke had explained to us at lunch that Chef Lou got involved in teaching at the Culinary Institute to help teach ex-GIs the culinary arts so they could secure a job after getting out of the service. Chef Lou had a heart for those in the military, as a veteran himself. I am sure he would be shocked to learn that over twenty-five years later, his biological son (whom he never met) would be one of those ex-GIs, walking the halls of the school, greeting professors as they walked by in their white coats and tall toques, learning the culinary arts in hopes of landing a job after being discharged.

"You have to call Ricky as soon as we get home," Kim said, startling me from my thoughts. This would not be like any of the other times we spoke. I felt like I was a kid on Christmas rushing to tell his best friend about all the gifts Santa brought.

"It wasn't any of the Caruso brothers, or even Duke," I told him anxiously. "It was HIS father, Louis." I gave him a minute to take this news in. "Chef Louis is OUR father!"

I shared every detail from the luncheon and tried my best to retell all the stories Duke, Edna, and Jeannine shared about our father. I told him our father owned the restaurant on Amsterdam Road, about getting the strange phone call from the hospital, about him closing the restaurant and making his way out to Indiana soon after I was born.

"Wow. Duke remembered that phone call? How wild is that?" Ricky said.

I could tell Ricky was just as excited to hear this information as I was to share it. He now knew in his midfifties, and after decades of searching, who his father was.

My heart was full that I was able to be a part of that. He was piecing his part of the story together, too. After that, every time I spoke to Ricky to give him new updates, he had more information for me. It was like we were completing a puzzle together, seven hundred miles apart.

Ricky and his wife had originally begun their search for his birth mother in 2018. Once the state of Indiana allowed birth records to be unsealed, they searched the Willard Library genealogy collections to seek the local history and any work records of his mom. Now that he learned of Chef Louis, they began looking for him in those same library directories. Ricky was able to find that in 1958, Chef Louis was listed as executive chef of the prestigious McCurdy Hotel in Evansville. The "Waldorf of the Midwest," if you will. They even found his address in the directory as Room #1A, McCurdy Hotel. Interestingly, Ricky was also able to track down his biological aunt, who informed him that his mother did, in fact, work at that same hotel, at the same time as Chef Louis, as a housekeeper and then working in the kitchen. She became pregnant, left her job, and entered a home for unwed mothers to give birth. And to no one's surprise, when they researched the directory in 1959, Chef Louis was no longer listed. No coincidence that they both worked together at the hotel in 1958, but as soon as she left to have Ricky in a home for unwed mothers, Johnny Appleseed was on the move again! I was beginning to sense a pattern here.

From the earliest days of the discovery, we would refer to each other on the phone or in texts as "brother," and continuously expressed that it was a blessing to find each other, even if late in life. Over the next several weeks, I made a point of meeting Duke for lunch or visiting him and Edna at their house. There were even times when Duke's younger brother Thomas would join us on video calls, and we'd pepper each other with question after question, craving any information about each other's childhoods, careers, and families. Duke was always forthcoming and was eager to answer all my questions about his upbringing and our father.

Duke was born Anthony Caruso, however, as a small child, he would run around the house declaring that he was "Duke of the house," so the name stuck. Duke shared stories about him and Edna being high school sweethearts, together for over sixty-five years. They had two children, Jeannine and Steven. Edna worked hard at home, taking care of both children and spending hours in the kitchen making the most delicious meals. Duke spent most of his career as the director of a facility providing guidance and counseling support for wayward boys. He also served as the assistant mayor in Johnstown. The more I learned about them, the more I saw that Duke and Edna had the ideal, hardworking, respectable, family-oriented relationship.

All this was still so fresh and new, and I couldn't help but panic the more I got to know these wonderful people. Why would they want to get to know me? Each day, I prepared myself for the "shoe to drop" and for them to say they wanted nothing to do with me. Once the "new puppy syndrome" wore off, would they have any need for me? As the weeks passed, we travelled through this new journey of brotherhood, sharing in long phone conversations, and Duke and I meeting at the local diner when we could. I couldn't help but fear that my new brothers and their families would get bored with me, and the novelty of our DNA discovery would wear off. It was all I had ever known, between my estranged relationship with my mother, becoming more distant with my siblings and even more distant with my stepsiblings. I was prepared and ready to be pushed aside, once again.

Sisters

For the past few weeks, I had also been calling, texting, and emailing all my siblings, cousins, and a few living aunts and uncles to inform them of my DNA test results. First and foremost, to let them know that I still loved them, and this new information changed nothing of our relationships. Secondly, to see if any one of them would have memories or information that would help me make sense of what may have transpired sixty-five years earlier.

My biggest fear was that one or more of my siblings would object to my accepting this new family and damage any already flimsy relationship.

As luck would have it, all my relatives were quite supportive of me. Truthfully, based on our memories, I don't think anyone found this to be that big of a surprise. Everyone knew my father was a womanizer, with rumors of infidelity. Yet, it was still wild to find out that my mother had a fling so soon after marrying my father, despite having three young children at home. Furthermore, to keep it a secret all this time was just mind-blowing. Of all her faults, and she had many, this was not anything we thought she would do.

One night, my sisters and I headed to Laurie's house so we could share stories to hopefully find clues as to how this happened. We all brought some food and had a nice dinner outside on a patio table. It was a lovely spring night, calm and very quiet sitting by the garage and surrounded by smells of the early perennials. We had never gotten together like this since being separated as children, other than a few holiday events in recent years. Knowing the conversation ahead of us, I wished our brothers could have been there, too. I felt flush as I prepared to start off the discussion. I knew we all felt a loss, learning that we were all now only half brothers and sisters, so I reiterated the fact that this would have no effect on our love for each other. I also reminded each of them of how grateful I was for their willingness to meet, knowing that it was going to be an inquisition of my mother and would definitely stir up some unwanted memories from our past. I didn't have anything planned or specific questions written out, so we just randomly chatted and tried to find some common memories that would possibly help make sense of it all. Toni, being the oldest, had more specific memories of our childhood, as did Laurie. Debbie could not (or would not let herself) remember much. Rae Ann, who was four years younger than me and quite young during our most tumultuous years, had suppressed all memories of her time with our parents at the big house. However, if Butchy were still alive, I know he would have had a lot to say.

We spoke of the huge property and the times we all got in trouble for one thing or another. No one could remember too many good times or specific presents they received for Christmas or birthdays, but we all remembered being on the Freddie Freihofer show, and Gram taking us downtown to watch the Christmas parade.

"Do you ever remember there being an Italian restaurant across the street from the big house?" I asked. Debbie and Rae Ann were not born then, so they would have had no memories of the building prior to it becoming a firehouse. Laurie couldn't recall either, but she would have only been two years old.

"Yes! There was a restaurant there before it became a firehouse," Toni said. "I only remember this because I remember Mom working there as a waitress." She paused. "Come to think of it, I'm pretty sure Dad would go over to play the drums some nights, too."

"Were Dad and Mom together during this time?" I inquired. "Like, she had to get a job because Dad was not around or providing?"

"Oh gosh, they were together then apart, then together again so many times. How am I supposed to remember!" she said, with a somewhat humorous tone.

They went out a lot because my father was always playing drums somewhere on the weekends, but up to that point, I assumed she was just a barfly who would dress up to go out and sit at the bar drinking and smoking while my father played. I had no idea that she was ever a waitress before I was born. Everyone who has ever worked in the restaurant business knows the sexual magnetism between cooks and waitresses. My mind went immediately to the potential, and cringy, scenarios. Did they have a few shift drinks before he lured her into his one-room travel trailer, which was parked directly behind the restaurant? Did this man take advantage of my mother, knowing she was going through tough times at home? Did she sneak him over into her house when my father was not around? Or, worse yet, was I conceived in what's commonly known now as a "canned ham" that Duke said was in the back of the restaurant for the many nights his father did not make it home? Did he take advantage of her and force himself on her with a few drinks, and it was a onetime mistake? The more I thought about it, the more I realized that the raunchy details didn't matter. No one would ever know the truth. But it all made sense to me now.

"Wait, so Dad was banging the drums while Mom was banging the chef?" I said, trying to lighten the mood.

"Tell us about your new brothers," Toni said.

"Duke is a wonderful man. They live in Johnstown. He has been married to Edna for fifty-plus years. She's this sweet Italian grandmother. They have a daughter in Ballston Spa. Then there's Ricky in Indiana and another brother Thomas in Columbus. He was born after Chef Lou closed the restaurant and moved to Evansville. Chef Louis appears to be a scoundrel but became a renowned chef." I tried to fill them in on everything we knew up until that point.

"But it's Chef Louis that I need to learn more about," I said, waiting for any negative reaction. There was none, meaning they understood my need to find out more about this man who was my biological father.

As the conversation continued, Toni and Laurie brought up different little nuggets of information that helped me piece together the timeline as well as sharpen my memory. We chatted about many things and had some laughs. No one wanted it to get too serious and critical of our parents. To be honest, I almost avoided asking more questions and purposely tried to steer away from becoming too uncomfortable. It was a wonderful night reminiscing and spending time with my sisters, and I truly hope they enjoyed it as much as I did.

However, there had to be someone who had answers. I was frantic to contact any living relative who would have been around during that period, who could possibly shed any light on the relationship between my mother and Chef Louis. I couldn't stop thinking about whether my father was aware of their relationship, and more importantly, did my father know I wasn't his? My sisters met with my Uncle Roland and his wife, who were good friends of my parents back then and always kept in touch, but they couldn't recall anything specific besides their continuous rocky relationship. Same went for my Aunt Donna. She was my mother's considerably younger half sister but wasn't around my mother too much through those years. I rattled my brain to think of who else would have witnessed that part of my parents' life.

Suddenly, I was hit with an intense wave of sadness. It finally occurred to me who would have known something: Gram. She knew everything that happened between them. She was so attuned to their relationship, and although she didn't always interfere with their feelings and situations, she definitely was aware of what went on. But would she have known this secret and not told anyone? Or did she know and chose not to tell anyone to protect me? Gram would have done anything to keep any of us kids safe and happy.

I felt like I was thumbing through a rolodex from beyond the grave. Anyone who was around during those years, like my father, Gram, or Aunt Lois and Uncle Bill, had already passed away, leaving me to search for clues through family stories and pictures. I ended up reaching out to Linda Hartje, the daughter of Aunt Lois and Uncle Bill.

"I know this is a long shot, but did you ever hear of your parents making comments about my mother not being faithful?" I asked over the phone.

"I'm sorry, Bill. I had no idea," Linda said, as she tried to recall any story or conversation that would have made sense to my mother's secret life choices.

The more we spoke, the more defeated I felt. Not just because I was running into constant dead ends instead of getting any answers, but I felt this overwhelming sense of guilt. I began excessively apologizing to her, as if she were her parents, as if I were in confession seeking some form of forgiveness. People often underestimate how difficult it is to stir up the past to heal childhood wounds. There I stood, in the back of the club, hiding near the bushes on my phone, weeping uncontrollably.

"I'm so sorry for not keeping in touch with them," I told her through the tears. "I never got to thank them for what they did for me. They were so kind and loving and I never got the chance to tell them how much I loved them and appreciated everything they did for me."

"They knew. They knew you loved them and boy, did they love you," Linda reassured me.

I never could see it at the time, but Aunt Lois and Uncle Bill did more for me than I could have ever imagined. Not only did they change my life by caring for my personal well-being during some of the most difficult times of my childhood, but they were able to show me that there was a better life out there than how life was with my parents. I'll never forget the compassion, strength, and warm-heartedness they showed. The constant motivation I have to make sure my family has a better life and to break my generational dysfunction is truly due to the testimony of their character. I will never forget them.

A few weeks later, Debbie invited me to her house to go through papers and documents that she was safekeeping along with some jewelry while my mother was in the nursing home. I knew Debbie supported me wanting to find out more about my past, but I was sure she was saddened for me, too. We were the closest in age and I couldn't help thinking that due to all this, she might have questioned who her father was, as well. I assured her that it really wasn't possible, since Louis closed the restaurant and left town by the end of the year. After hearing Duke talk about Louis and his time at the restaurant, it was obvious he didn't hang around long enough even for me to be brought home from the hospital, let alone for them to continue their relationship. Debbie really had nothing to worry about. She was so much like my mother, with fair skin and freckles, and had many other shared physical and emotional features similar to my father that left little doubt as to who her parents were. Truthfully, I'm glad she never wanted to take a test of her own.

She pulled out some boxes of jewelry, keepsakes, and documents that she did not want left at the nursing home with our mother. We read through many back-and-forth attorney letters and custody judgements in yellowed envelopes mixed in with dozens of love letters my mother had saved in a small box. Most were from my father to her, beginning with "Hi Hon" and ending with "Love Always, Bill." It was a strange feeling to hear them being civil to each other. My father expressed concern for how she was doing and how much he loved her in every letter he sent. My throat became dry and my eyes welled up. Others were her replying to him and full of similar sentiments. I scoured these letters written in the summer of 1962 when she was in the hospital. With each handwritten word, it was evident that they still loved each other at that time. Yes, their relationship was complicated, tumultuous, and they often struggled to see eye to eye, however these letters showed their true feelings for each other, and how their love and affection for one another was pure. There was nothing in these letters that alluded to infidelity, lack of trust, or more importantly, any morsel of information about Chef Louis or her secret. So, if the father that raised me truly had no idea that she was unfaithful, what happened between the fall of '62 and when they finally divorced in '65? Plus, there were no letters from any of her other husbands, just my father. They obviously loved each other throughout the years, maybe even at different times, yet in their infamous love-hate relationship, they couldn't fight it any longer, and hate won out.

Sunday Dinner

Jeannine had arranged for our families to get together in early April, at one of Schenectady's oldest and most respected Italian restaurants, Cornells, one of Duke's favorites. I was just as nervous and anxious as I was before our first luncheon meeting, but this time I was excited, too, like taking my first flight. Having my wife and children with me this time was more relaxing, and I was really looking forward to introducing my immediate family to Duke and his.

Kim, Billy, Brad, Courtney, and I arrived at the restaurant about the same time as Duke and Edna were walking in. I spotted Duke right away as he and Edna waited at the top of the ramp entering the restaurant. I felt such a mix of joy and pride when I saw Duke's loving smile. He beelined towards me, going in for one of his famous hugs, topped with a kiss on my cheek.

"It is so good to see you again, brother," he said.

"Duke, I'd like you to meet my children. My sons Billy and Brad, and my daughter Courtney." I watched as my newly found half brother embraced each one of my kids in such a loving way, as if he had known them their whole life. It seemed surreal to have my family meet Duke. I still had moments in which it didn't seem real, that the father who raised me wasn't my biological father, and now I knew who that man actually was. Getting to know Duke was the closest I would get to knowing my father. And Duke's genuine personality and kindness definitely made this wild situation much more comfortable.

After a few moments of introductions and hugs, we were escorted to a private room in which we all gathered around a large table. Duke and I, again, sat next to each other flanked by our supportive spouses. Jeannine and her husband Dave were quite social, as were my three children, and everyone was soon conversing with intermittent laughter. Dave brought his unique ability to converse with everyone and make them feel comfortable. He and Billy ended up ordering the exact same meal, right down to the dessert. This made that entire end of the table giggle all night, as if they had known each other for years.

Duke kept reaching out and holding my hand, and I don't think he, or I for that matter, stopped smiling the entire evening. We spoke of our families and how amazing it had been these past few months since finding each other. We shared stories about telling the other people in our life and how truly wild it was that we found each other after all this time. Courtney joked that next year, she was only going to get me an umbrella for Christmas, as getting me this whole extra family was a little extreme. The whole table roared with laughter.

One of the sweetest moments of the night was when Billy took my iPad and was able to connect to Ricky via Skype. We passed the iPad around and everyone introduced themselves to Ricky,

Cindy, and their daughter Becky. They were able to be a part of this moment, too, thanks to technology. As the iPad hopped around, I glanced at Duke. I was quickly learning that he was much more emotional than I was, so it was no surprise that he struggled to hold back his tears as we were able to visually meet Ricky and include them in this family gathering. We all shared this experience in different ways. Finding out about me reminded Duke of his father's faults and infidelity and how his mother was treated. Ricky found out who his biological parents were and was able to fill a void that had haunted him for decades. I, unbeknownst to me, had a different biological father that no one knew of, and in turn, lost a father and grandmother who I adored. But, through this process, we all gained three brothers and expanded all our families.

As our evening wrapped up, I looked for the server to make sure I was able to pick up the tab. It was just something that I always did, no matter who I was with or where I was. I am not sure why. Perhaps deep down, it is my way of showing that I have found success and with that, I can provide for others, or perhaps, growing up hungry, I felt that food represented love. There had been an odd comfort when Duke told me at our lunch that our father did the same.

"It's been taken care of already," the waitress told me.

I looked down at the other end of the table. Dave grinned and gave a shrug. Son of a gun! Nevertheless, nothing could frustrate me after a night like this. A table full of empty dessert plates and wine glasses, conversations still lingering, and newly found family members hugging goodbye and making plans for our next get-to-gether. As I stared out into this room, I could only feel grateful.

Independence Day

Albany Country Club sits just outside of Albany in the Helder-bergs, with majestic views looking down over the city. One of the most anticipated events each year, with upwards of twelve hundred members and guests in attendance, is our Independence Day celebration in July. The club is fortunate enough to have their own permit and is able to shoot fireworks straight up over the large pond on the eighth hole, providing a fantastic view of the display that is practically right overhead.

For many years, I wouldn't think of inviting family to my place of work. I was just never comfortable with my worlds intersecting. I remember one time, my father and Marge drove out to Ohio on the spur of the moment to visit us. He had just purchased a new beautiful van and wanted to take a long drive. We had just purchased a three-bedroom ranch with the GI Bill, with a ten percent mortgage rate when everyone else was paying upwards of eighteen percent. (I knew those nights in Germany as a tower rat would pay off one day.) The house had a large, fenced yard that backed up into acres and acres of corn or soybeans, whichever was planted that year. It was the typical rural, Midwest set up. We were so happy they could come see us, especially since this was the first time they were able to meet our daughter, Courtney. It was so lovely to be with them, as we sat around the backyard looking out into the fields, while the kids played. In hindsight, this was also an emotional visit as it would be the last time I would see Marge before she passed.

But then they wanted to see where I worked. I remember feeling such anxiety as we all piled in his van and drove to the club. I couldn't imagine having my family around my place of work. I became increasingly flush and felt almost faint as we drove around the parking lot. The last thing I wanted to do was invite them inside. So, they got a wonderful tour of the parking lot where I pointed out the pool and tennis areas. Debbie and Larry also made a drive out with their kids the following summer and they, too, never saw the inside of the clubhouse. I never could decide whether it was embarrassment or my anxiety, knowing I lived with some elements of imposter syndrome. I knew they had no idea of the difference in my two worlds and that for me to succeed in one, I had to bury the old.

However, over the last several years at Albany Country Club, my walls had come down and I would invite Debbie, Larry, their kids, and now several grandchildren to enjoy the festivities, including bounce houses, balloons, cotton candy, and face painting. Since they had a large group, we always seated them in the ballroom which had more large tables to accommodate bigger families. Although I was still a bit uncomfortable mixing my worlds, they just blended into the crowd of over twelve hundred people and no one knew who they were.

This year was different. This year, I also wanted to invite Duke, Edna, Jeannine, and Dave to show off where we worked, and felt like there was no better event for it. Kim seated them at an open table on our Albany Room patio, which was at the end of the building, but had one of the best views of the fireworks. They were seated right alongside several of my members who request that patio every year, knowing that it was one of the club's "best kept secrets" for watching the fireworks. I could tell that some of our "regulars" were beginning to look and wonder who these new folks were. Without any embarrassment or hesitation, I was proud to introduce Duke as my half brother.

"Mr. and Mrs. Young," I said, "I'd like to introduce you to my half brother Duke and his wife Edna." Mr. Young was one of my past presidents and we had a comfortable working relationship. He was the club's consummate ambassador, a kind-hearted soul always there to support me and my family.

"What a pleasure it is to meet you!" Mr. Young said, as he shook their hands.

I introduced the rest of the members on that patio to my family. This was the first time in my career that I introduced any of my siblings or relatives, besides my wife and children, to my members. This was so out of character for me. I would have crawled under the table before letting longtime members see into my private world. Through the years, we had hosted several of my nieces' and nephews' weddings at the club, but they were separated so the members never knew who the wedding was for.

With Duke and Edna now welcomed comfortably on their patio, I went down into the ballroom to talk to Debbie and Larry.

"Come with me," I said, "I want you to meet Duke and Edna."

I could tell Debbie was nervous, but I walked them over to the outer patio and introduced them. Duke was his usual charming, loving, embracing self, and put Debbie at ease immediately. She could see I was proud of my new family and what a sweet couple they were. I spent the rest of the evening enjoying their company and the fireworks. This was also the first time in the last few years that I stayed for the whole show. Usually, I left Kim and the staff to handle the cleanup and would be home listening to the fireworks from my house. A weight was lifted for me at that moment. It was so important to me that they met, and even more critical that I let them all know that I was not deserting my current siblings for new ones, just expanding the family. Maybe that's why I was not insecure or nervous about them all being there together in view of my members. I just felt lucky.

Golden Toque

Throughout the next few weeks, Duke and I would often meet for brunch at the Blue Ribbon—one of the oldest diners in Schenectady. Although we usually met midweek, the place always had a steady flow of people, and we would watch the servers work tirelessly to turn their tables throughout the afternoon. On this particular day, Duke was waiting for me just inside the front foyer when I arrived. I'll never forget how his face lit up with the most genuine smile as soon as I entered.

"How ya doing, brother?" he asked as he pulled me in, giving me a big hug.

"Good," I responded. "It's so good to see you. How's Edna?"

He'd recently told us that Edna was having some health issues, and his daughter, Jeannine, was helping with doctor visits and making healthy dinners for them. Edna was an excellent cook, but she had to watch what she ate, which meant going easy on the Italian feasts.

This was only the third or fourth time that we had gotten together, individually or as a family, but the bond we shared was so unique. We stumbled upon some buried secrets from the past, and, luckily for us, we forged a strong connection. Duke is a lover. He has loved his beautiful wife, Edna, since they first met at seventeen. He loves his family like no one I have ever met. He loves his relationship with God, but most importantly, he truly loves himself. The more I got to know Duke, the more our relationship made sense. He didn't have to answer that phone call, he didn't have to meet with me in Johnstown that day, and most importantly, he didn't need to love me as a brother. But he does. His compassion and understanding for those he loves is rare. During some of our weekly Zoom calls, Ricky would join, and when we would ask about including Duke's brother Tim, Duke would calmly inform us that he was taking the idea of secret brothers that show up sixty years later a little harder. "He just needs some time...We'll get together soon. Just need to be patient."

We were directed to our table at the far end of the elongated row of booths. I let Duke walk in front of me, only to notice him holding another manila envelope, just like the one he gave me at our first meeting. I assumed it was additional pictures of our father that he wanted to share with me. Once we settled in at the table, I anxiously fumbled with my menu and unrolled my utensils wrapped in that tiny paper napkin; however, chatting with Duke was effortless. It was like we had known each other for years. He spoke to me with sincerity and compassion, knowing that I was dealing with the realization that the last sixty-five years of my life was a lie, on top of grieving the loss of my father and grandmother who raised me. He shared stories of his father with affection blended with some intense honesty.

"He was no saint!" Duke admitted. "He was not the best father or family man." His voice cracked as he opened up about our father. "He was who he was," he added. "He was my father, and I have and always will love him."

I picked up the huge menu to hide the fact that my eyes were filling with tears. Luckily, the server came back over, and we ordered our sandwiches. This distracted us for a moment and allowed me a minute to process how Duke was speaking about Lou. As hard as this news had been for me, I hadn't thought about how it was affecting Duke. Even after finding two brothers that he went his whole life without knowing, he could still speak of how he loved his father without an ounce of resentment.

As the server collected our menus, Duke reached over on the seat beside him and opened that manila envelope. I was anxiously waiting to see more pictures of this man who I share DNA with. The last few weeks had been an intense roller coaster of emotions as I learned more and more about Lou and his life. After seeing his picture in full chef whites, I'd been grappling with the idea of not only this man being my father, but my father being a successful culinarian—a career that I'd worked so hard at and respected immensely. Duke reached inside the envelope and carefully pulled out two beautiful medals. I recognized those medals instantly. I had spent hours staring at that eight by ten glossy photograph of Chef Louis that he gave me at our first lunch. I knew every detail of that photo, so it was without hesitation that I knew exactly what he was showing me.

"Our dad would want you to have these," he said softly, as tears filled his eyes.

I couldn't respond. It felt like my body froze as Duke handed the medals to me. There were no words I could come up with at that moment to sincerely express how I felt. These medals were more than just his culinary awards, his prized possessions. They were a piece of my father. As I held the medals in my shaking hands, I looked at Duke, with tears now flowing down both of our faces.

"No way. These are too special to you and your family," I stated, as I tried to hand them back. But Duke was adamant.

"Don't be silly!" he said, pushing away my arm. "He would want you to have these. Of all his sons, he would want you to have the culinary medals that meant so much to him."

I held onto the medals tight, my fingers tracing every detail like I had just lost my sight and was using braille for the first time. My finger slid over each number and letter scratched on the back. Holding these medals was bittersweet. On the one hand, I felt honored and special to have something of his, something that I knew he was proud of and treasured immensely. On the other hand, accepting these medals now meant that I accepted him. That I accepted him as my father and somehow now needed to forgive him for knowing I existed yet never looking back. Truthfully, I hadn't fully decided how I felt about the Artful Dodger and his Johnny Appleseed behaviors. I gently slid the medals back into the plastic bag that Duke brought them in, so old and discolored I could tell it was the original bag that Chef Louis had kept them in.

When I got home that afternoon, I immediately began my research on these medals and the Order of the Golden Toque. Many chefs during that time formed organizations and developed awards to promote the culinary arts; however, only a few were recognized by the entire industry, such as the American Culinary Federation and Michelin stars. I was determined to learn more about Chef Louis's accomplishments within the culinary world I was familiar with. If I were to accept this man as part of my life, I wanted to know everything I could. I pulled the medals back out of that old, stained bag. I retraced the "1961" and "Caruso" struck on the back. My mind raced through everyone and anyone who might have been around during that time and would have any idea of the details of this award. I thought of all the different mentors and chefs that I'd worked for and with over the years, but truthfully, I blanked with coming up with anyone.

"Why don't you give Yono a call? If he doesn't know, maybe he could give you the name of someone who might," Kim suggested from the living room couch. She was curled on the couch, reading on her tablet. Without even picking her head up, she was my voice of reason from the adjoining room.

Of course, Yono would know something! Yono Purnomo is a certified executive chef who immigrated to the US from Indonesia, and has cooked, competed, and educated all over the world. Not only is he an expert in the culinary field, but his philanthropic efforts are unmatched. He will never say no to any charity organization or event that could use his help as a celebrity chef, even setting up his own charity giving promising young Indonesian chefs an opportunity to work in the US in an exchange program. He is listed in "Best Chefs America," and we in the Capital Region are lucky enough to have his restaurant in the heart of Albany. His wife, Donna, works alongside him, as well as his son Dominick. When we spoke, there was a mutual camaraderie of managing the restaurant business with our families. My thumb quickly scrolled through my contacts on my phone until I found Yono.

"Hey, Chef, how have you been?" I asked. I always referred to anyone in the field as "chef" as a term of respect.

"Bill! So good to hear from you! What's going on, my friend?" he replied most genuinely.

"Well, actually, a lot! I won't get into it now, but my life has been shaken up a bit lately. But I have a random question for you. Have you ever heard of an organization called The Order of the Golden Toque?" I asked, my heart feeling like it would burst from my chest. I so desperately needed him to know more about this.

"Of course!" he replied quickly. "I am a member!" As soon as the words came out of his mouth, I felt such relief. I had known and admired Yono for many years, so hearing that he not only knew of this culinary organization but was a part of it was reassuring. I shared my story about discovering that my biological father was a chef and how I ended up with these medals.

"Wow, I guess we now know where you got your restaurant genes from!" he said through a chuckle. We exchanged pleasantries and said we would see each other at the next ROC meeting. The ROC was a restaurant cooperative buying group of which Chef Yono and I were both on the board of directors. After we hung up, an intense sense of pride rose inside me. If Chef Louis was in an elite league with the likes of culinarians like Chef Yono, then how could I not admire him as a great chef who achieved great things, despite walking away from his son?

So, I returned to the computer to dig deeper into this award's beginnings and find out if anyone alive may recognize the name, Chef Louis Caruso. I googled The Order of the Golden Toque, and immediately found their website. The "Golden Toque," which means the golden chef's hat, was founded in France and brought to the United States by Chef Pierre Berard. It was registered in the US Patent Office as The Honorable Order of the Golden Toque in 1961. It is the *highest acclaimed recognition a chef can receive in America.* According to their website, recognition goes to chefs with more than twenty years of service, who demonstrated professional attainment of the highest degree, abiding interest in professional progress, and devoted and distinguished service to the culinary profession and arts. Membership is restricted to one hundred lifetime members. I located a page on their site that listed the contact information for their current board of governors. My first call was to the association, who directed me to the current acting secretary and historian, an executive chef at a hotel in Frankenmuth, Michigan.

He was kind enough to contact me the next day. I summarized my story and told him I was looking for verification of these medals. He said he would be happy to look into it. I was pleasantly surprised that an executive chef of a massive hotel in Michigan with many responsibilities would take the time to get back to me only after a few days to confirm. Chef Wurzel looked into the historical records and told me Louis Caruso was, in fact, a part of the first hundred founding honorees. Chef Louis Caruso was honored with this prestigious award as one of the original hundred members in 1961.

Now what? I thought. Was I supposed to admire this man just because he was adorned with these medals? Could I even justify our connection? Was it superficial of me to consider accepting him as my father solely because I had compassion and understanding for someone who achieved greatness in the brutal culinary world? Or, did I ignore the shimmer and shine of his accolades due to the fact that he chose success over me, and all his achievements were at the expense of his family and (at least) two illegitimate offspring along the way? At this point, I was confident that the father who raised me had no idea I was not his, as he passed the name of William Aperance to me. I honestly could not imagine he would have done such a thing if he knew that I was not his. So, maybe it was for the best that Chef Louis never reached out to me. Could you imagine if he did? It would have only made things worse between my parents, and it could have actually prevented my three younger siblings from even being born. Should I applaud him for that? Did my mother have the smallest amount of compassion and hide this secret from us not to save herself but to preserve the family that she was desperately trying to hold on to? This was hard to believe, as history showed she was not emotionally stable enough to think of any future ramifications and could only think of herself.

I grew up in the business. I went to the same culinary school that he taught at twenty years earlier. I worked my butt off in the same industry he thrived in. I knew the commitment, grind, and toll it took on someone. It was impossible not to feel some connection to this man. The medals were physical proof of that bond that would connect us further without ever meeting. I once came across this idea in the work of Morgan Harper Nichols: What if everything connects? What if the person you choose to be ends up having ripple effects in years to come in the life of someone you'll never meet?

Questioning My Mother

With all this new information backing up the DNA revelation, I was flooded with numerous questions. The more I spoke with my siblings and family, the more I realized that the only adult living who could provide me with the truth was, in fact, my mother. Memoirist Adrienne Brodeur stated, "To keep the truth buried, you must tend to it." My mother had tended to this secret for my entire life.

She had moved to Florida with her fifth husband until he passed away. When she became less independent, Toni moved her to a home closer to her in South Carolina and was able to take care of her as best she could. Ironically, the child that my mother berated, emotionally abused, and beat until she couldn't take it anymore, and who was kicked out of the house at seventeen with just a suitcase, walking down the four-lane highway in the middle of the night, would be the one who would take care of her in her old age. Recently, Toni moved back to New York to be closer to her children, which led to transferring my mother to a nursing home facility locally. This gave all my siblings the opportunity to visit her, occasionally, except Laurie and me. Our relationship had deteriorated and I had not spoken to her in decades. I never visited her in Florida or when she came up to New York. I would go back and forth sometimes, wondering whether my estrangement was justified or if I was just being stubborn. Would I regret not making amends, before it was too late? Did we deserve to make amends? As the years passed, the thought of mending any fence with her became nearly impossible.

However, at this moment, I needed to at least attempt to see if she would be willing to provide me with some answers. Even if that meant I would have to face her. My siblings and I could only put together little bits and pieces based on our scattered and meager memories. Despite our relationship, or lack thereof, I believed she owed me this. She had buried my truth and had tended to it for the last sixty-five years. And now here I stood with a shovel.

Debbie knows me better than I know myself sometimes. She knew that talking to my mother would be quite a feat, so she offered to pick her brain a little before I built up the courage to speak to her. Debbie would do anything for her family, despite the uneasy feelings or anxiety it might cause her, especially if my mother confessed anything.

"Ask her if she remembers an Italian restaurant on Amsterdam Road. Maybe that will trigger her to come clean," I told Debbie on the phone, as she was getting ready to head out for a visit to the nursing home.

When she got there, she decided to take a roundabout approach, since she did not have much to go on at this point. "Hey, Ma...I received a phone call from an Italian man asking for you," she said nervously.

My mother may have been ninety, but she was still sharp as a tack. "What was his name?" she asked.

This caught my sister off guard, and she quickly responded, "Um, he didn't give me his name."

They sat there silently for a moment, Debbie thought for sure that she was about to break and spill the beans. Just then, my mother quipped back, "Well, then how do you know he was Italian?"

Even if she was vague and the question was not asked or answered clearly, I felt my mother was sharp enough to wonder why Debbie was inquiring. Debbie knew this was going nowhere and changed the subject.

A few weeks later, I was still dragging my feet and was not ready to face my mother, so I swallowed my pride and asked my sisters if they would maybe show her the picture I had of him. I assured them that if they were uncomfortable doing this, I would be willing to go with them and face her directly. They knew how important this was to me and agreed to take care of it. I provided the picture of Chef Louis in full chef whites as he would have looked in the sixties and sent them with a few questions. *Did my father that raised me know that he was not my biological father? Did anyone know but her?* I knew that she must have known Chef Louis was my father by the phone call to the restaurant, which I believed with all my heart was remembered accurately and truthfully by Duke. The picture would have been less than ten years after she last saw him. She would have to recognize him.

A few days later, my sisters Debbie and Rae Ann made a trip to the nursing home to spend the afternoon with their mother. As they looked back on the afternoon, they noted that my mother seemed tired, often fading in and out, but she was still quite coherent. My sisters spent most of the time there anxiously coming up with anything else in the world to talk to her about besides me and my newly found father.

"Michael is doing really well at his new job in Florida. I'm sure it's hot down there though. I can't imagine all that humidity," Debbie said, as she refolded the newspaper and placed it nice and neat on the table near my mother's bed. Chef Louis's picture lay face down, directly next to the pile. With every piece of newspaper, she placed down, she stared at the back of his picture, almost worried that it was going to jump right off that table and into her lap.

"It looks like the grounds crew finally mowed around here," Rae said, anxiously looking out the window.

"Yep," my mother said softly, as she closed her eyes, preparing to take her midafternoon nap. Debbie knew she would have to do it soon. It was closing in on late afternoon and it became obvious that they couldn't stall much longer. Her hands moist with anticipation, Debbie opened the envelope and slid out that glossy eight by ten photo of the man my mother had a secret affair with. Trembling slightly, she held out the picture.

"Ma? Do you know this man?" she asked. "Do you remember spending time with him? He was a chef."

My sisters stayed silent as she gazed at the picture, slightly tracing the lines of his face with her delicate, frail fingers. It was as if time froze in the room. Actually, it was as if they went back in time, to January 1954. Back to that busy Italian restaurant's kitchen...

"Chef, I need to fire those meatballs for table sixteen. They raved about the food last week and now they're getting antsy because it's taking too long!" she yelled across the hotline, making sure she was heard over the sounds of slamming pots and pans.

"They'll be done in a minute, darling. Wouldn't want to make a pretty gal like you wait," he tossed back, flirtatiously, giving a wink and flashing his charming, sweet smile.

There my mother stood, back in that kitchen, staring longingly at that man behind the hotline. The man who gave her all the attention and satisfaction that she so desperately craved. The man she would sneak off with after a shift, while the father that raised me would be packing up his drum set from that same shift, in that same restaurant. The man who knocked her up but then took off, never to be seen again. Until now...

"Ma?" Debbie said as she nudged my mother softly on the shoulder, as if to wake her up from her dream. She jumped as if she had been startled, and looked at each of my sisters, and then back at the picture. Without saying a word, she slowly turned her head and gazed out the window, her eyes becoming heavier. Despite receiving no answers or information, my sisters felt she was too tired, and that it would be best if they did not press her on this, at least not anymore today. They each leaned in for their customary kisses and said goodbye.

Kim and I were in a board meeting at the club until around eight p.m. that night. When the meeting broke, we went back to our respective offices and saw that both of our phones were filled with texts and missed calls from Debbie and Toni. My mother had passed away just hours after they left. I stood there, motionless. I couldn't move, even if I wanted to. She fucking died.

Denial

Grief is a funny thing. They say it comes in stages: denial, anger, bargaining, depression, acceptance. If you were to have told me at any point in the previous forty-five years that I would grieve the loss of my mother, I probably wouldn't have believed you. For me, there was nothing to grieve for. I had moved on and created a wonderful life that did not include her. My wife and children had no relationship or connection to her. I had just made it a point in my life to move on from my past, and the only way I knew how to do that was by leaving her in it. Being a parent, I have learned—sometimes the hard way—that my children's well-being will drive every decision I make. I worked my ass off for many years just to make sure they did not suffer the trauma and neglect that I did. I live and breathe for my family. My mother didn't. As I reflect on any memories I have of and with her, I cannot remember a single time in which her choices supported me or were for my benefit.

So, of course, she would die just a few hours after seeing Chef Louis's picture. I closed my office door, slumped into my desk chair, and just sat there. What the actual fuck? She died. No way did she freaking die. My sisters went to see if she would admit to knowing who my father was, and she died. She looked at his picture, rolled over, and died. How did this happen? Did seeing his picture have anything to do with her passing? Did she know she was about to be called out on her lifelong secret, which caused her blood pressure to rise? Holy shit! Did I kill her? Just two weeks earlier, she was sharp enough mentally to ask Debbie, "What was his name?" when asked about "some Italian guy." Fuck. I mean, I guess it was slightly poetic that she was gone, and I was left angry, disappointed, and empty. In hindsight, this was our entire relationship. Once again, she let me down when I needed her the most. Once again, she couldn't provide me with what I needed. Once again, her selfishness won out, taking my truth and all the secrets she kept with it right to the grave. All I needed from her was to provide any information so I wasn't left with so many unanswered questions, but she couldn't even do that for me. Did I just want her to admit it? Did I want an apology? Or, frankly, did I want to stick it to her? Her dirty little secret had been busted open like a jack-in-the-box, slowly cranked for over sixty years. At this point, my reasoning became irrelevant. I got up from my chair and left my office, slamming the door behind me. I made my way down the hall and pushed out the front door. I guess all I wanted was some justification for my part in our estranged relationship, I thought, as I made my way to my car. I peeled out of that lot as if I had left a cloud of dust in my wake. As vindicated as I felt, man, was I pissed.

My Mother's Service

"Are you sure you don't want to go?" Kim asked, knowing what my answer would be. She was already dressed and was digging through her purse to find her car keys.

I was in my sweatpants, settled in on the couch, and had still not taken a shower after working in the yard. "Nah, everyone knows we haven't spoken in decades. It would be hypocritical for me to show up, and no one expects me to be there," I muttered. "I'll reach out to them individually and give my condolences." I barely lifted my head off the couch cushion.

"Alright, but are you sure you won't mind if I do go?" she asked again before she headed out the door.

"Nope," I muttered, knowing she planned on going regardless of what I said.

Truthfully, it was good that she was going. We both knew that if she went, she would come home and give me a detailed account of who was there and what was said during the eulogy. I may not have spoken to my mother in over four decades, but that didn't mean I wasn't curious about the event.

I heard the car leave and thought I would take a nap. We had both taken the day off work even though I knew I wouldn't attend the service. With my head buried in a couch cushion, I began to question my mother and *our* relationship, questioning my role in it. It was hard to sleep. I tried to get all the thoughts out of my mind. Was I to blame? Why did I avoid her and become estranged for so long? It wasn't hatred, I thought to myself. I never really thought I loved her, so how could it have been hatred? It started out that I was just pissed at her, like any young teenager would be who went through what I did. Then it turned into "she's dead to me" after what I saw her do in later years. Then it turned into stubbornness, I guess, and I stuck to my guns. I felt I had a right to avoid her, and without any overture on her part, I wasn't budging. I guess, shamefully, I never had any desire to. As time went by, it became easier, and I thought of her less and less.

Even as a child, I felt estranged from her. She possibly resented my presence because I constantly reminded her of her secret. I will give her credit for not letting my father know of the affair or the secret, which would have certainly ended the relationship, and my younger three siblings may never have been born. Our father was not one for showering us with attention or expressing his emotions, but there was never any feeling that we were unwanted. I believed with every fiber of my body that he was my father. I looked like him and tried to emulate him in every way possible to gain his love and approval. Even if he knew and accepted it to save the marriage, he certainly could not have remained silent and not thrown it in my mother's face during their many arguments and fights.

I thought about how things may have been different. Would my life have been different? These thoughts made me more depressed. What if I did not avoid her? What if we had a strained but normal relationship? Would she have come clean? Would she have told me? I honestly don't think so. But I now had to wrestle with this question every day. What if she told me? I could have found him without the aid of Ancestry. It would have been a short trip to Columbus, I thought. To meet the man who was my biological father and get to meet him before his passing. I'm sure we would have hit it off, since we had much in common, career-wise. I would have had a million questions for him. Then again, she could have told me, and when I reached out to him, he could have denied it.

After a few hours, Kim returned from the service. I was reluctant to ask questions. Still, she knew I would want to know all about it, so before I could even say anything, she started in, "Well, that was interesting! I mean, that was kind of bizarre!" She began describing her experience. "I got there about ten minutes late, but the service hadn't started yet," she said. She shared how she met up with my niece's husband, Kevin, in the parking lot and that they chatted as they walked in together.

"I don't know why Bill even took that DNA test," he said. "I certainly wouldn't have done it or wouldn't want to know the results! You know, you spit in the tube, and then the damn government has you by the balls!" he said, half-joking, as they entered.

"Bill's situation was different," Kim said in my defense. "Once Billy's results returned with no one else on his father's side showing up with any Italian, he had to know."

They entered the funeral parlor lobby and were directed to the left side, where my mother's service was being held. Kim quickly scanned the room for my brother and sisters, who she was there for. With the small attendance, she quickly located my siblings, who were pleasantly surprised and grateful to see that she had come. "Thank you for coming," my sisters said as Kim hugged each of them. They knew I was not likely to be there, but they appreciated Kim coming just the same. Kim had maintained a lovely relationship with all my sisters over the years. She thought it was important to stay connected. This is another thing I love about Kim. Her kind heart. She would constantly remind me to "just stop avoiding them. They are your family." Kim was almost always right. Okay, *always* right! With Kim keeping us in contact, we had more opportunities to get together occasionally at a shower, birthday, or wedding in addition to the Aperance family Christmas dinner.

After chatting with them for a little while, the funeral service began, so Kim took a seat a few rows behind my siblings, who were sitting up in the front.

"How many people were there?" I asked.

"Hard to say?" She tried to count them all in her head. "There was a total of maybe forty, counting the grandchildren, but not many more, and most were just your brother, sisters, and their families," she said. "Oh yeah, Aunt Donna, Aunt Helen, and your cousins, the Straits." Neither of us was surprised that it would have been mostly my immediate family and very few others.

My jaw tightened, my throat became dry, and my nose began to tingle. *I'm not going to cry.* I imagined I was inside the room and seeing all the faces, thinking, remove the immediate family and who was there? Any close friends? Neighbors? Coworkers? I couldn't imagine any. Not that there weren't a few, but no one was close. All I saw were those familiar faces, who she treated so poorly, so often.

Kim explained that the service started about fifteen minutes after she arrived, so she didn't miss anything except a few people who came before, like my older sister Laurie, who had already come and gone. She was estranged from my mother for almost as long.

Kim continued sharing the details as she unloaded the dishwasher. I went over to give her a hand. "When I went up to the front, there was a booklet where, if you wanted, you could write something special that you remembered about her or something you will miss." Without even picking her head up from sorting the silverware, she said, "I just signed my name."

Kim went on to tell me that a middle-aged gentleman had come out and begun to give the eulogy. She knew him immediately to be the "house minister" of some denomination hired by the funeral home. From the moment she walked through the doors, she felt that there was something odd about this service, different from any other ones she attended. We had both attended many services of family, friends, and numerous members of our clubs. So, we both were no strangers to wakes and services. But this one was much different, and Kim noticed it right away.

"So, wait, no one spoke but the minister?" I asked.

"Yup," she answered. "I was surprised as well. None of the dozens of relatives there had anything to say or wanted to add to the prepared eulogy. It was just odd."

Kim listened intently to the carefully scripted eulogy as the minister spoke of my mother's early life as an adopted child, raised by her great-aunt and uncle who lived next door to her grandparents, and growing up as a child of privilege.

"He said she had an outgoing, vibrant personality, striking beauty as a young woman, and was a talented pianist. He spoke of her love of animals. But really, her love of dogs," Kim went on. "Then he surprisingly told us that some said she loved her dogs more than her children!" Since Kim was well aware of my upbringing, she thought this was telling and ironic. They all knew I would not be in attendance, so it wasn't as if the eulogy was written to spare my feelings or not upset me. That made it more striking that the decades of raising seven children with four husbands would not even get an honorable mention. I'm sure my sisters wanted to say nice things about her and not highlight those years. Kim told me then, "I quietly looked around the room to see if any others were experiencing the same uncomfortable feeling that this eulogy was incomplete, to say the least."

"Were there any pictures of us as kids? Or any with her during those years?" I asked.

"There was the usual collage of pictures, quickly collected by your sisters, that only included those as a young girl, none of you all growing up, several with her and the grandchildren, and the rest were her and Bud living in Florida." Kim grabbed her glass of wine as I finished wiping down the counter and followed her into the family room. Kim said her sympathy toward the small group quickly turned to curiosity. What happened to all the missing years? "I felt sure everyone in the room must have noticed it," she said. "I was suddenly overcome with this enormous feeling of pity that nothing good could have been said about any of her children and those missing years."

Her detailed description of the service and the oddity of it made me, for the first time in sixty-five years, no longer feel anger towards my mother, but a sense of sadness. Was I really feeling sorry for her?

Avoidance

It had never occurred to me that my mother's and my strained relationship was any bit my fault, but looking back, I can now see how I was partially to blame. I was stubborn. I was unwilling. I had no compassion for her or her mental health or for how she treated my siblings and me. I was resentful and had no interest in her feelings. Mainly because I knew she had zero interest in ours. We lived a tactile-less relationship. We ended up being around each other with no emotional connection. As a child, I could only assume it was because I was terrible, so I was left with the impression that she didn't want me because of that.

I'll never forget the time when I was struggling in elementary school. I was displaying clear signs of having severe emotional issues, such that a child nowadays would have instantly been recommended for professional counseling. I didn't speak to anyone outside of my siblings or family. I also moved from house to house and school to school amid all my parent's turmoil. This wasn't easy for a kid like me. So when the school notified my mother that I needed to repeat fifth grade, my mother ripped into the school in a tirade. Not to defend me whatsoever but to make sure the school knew it was my problem, and even their problem, but in no way, shape, or form was it her fault. But that's also how she treated the situation with her dogs and my rabbits. I was vulnerable, distraught, and upset, but she went out of her way to make it clear that she or her dogs were not to be blamed. The hatred I had built towards her was based on years of abandonment, physical and emotional abuse, and neglect.

The icing on the cake for me was when I was in high school, and I had come home to Gram's house from one of my dishwashing shifts at the Turf Tavern. As I drove up the driveway, I saw my little brother, Jeff, sitting on the back steps alone, with a grocery bag of his clothes. He was the only one who chose to live with our mother once our father and Marge rescued us from the shelter.

"What are you doing here?" I asked, knowing that it was a habit for all of us to make our way to Gram's house for respite.

"Mom and Chuck were fighting again. They told me to leave," he said, with a quiver in his voice.

After everything Jeff had been through, custody battles at a very young age, the relationship with Marge and my father, being split up from his siblings at such a young age, my mother fought for custody when Jeff needed her. But within a few years she had the audacity to side with a man over her child. This, to me, was unforgivable. When I became a father, my brain couldn't even process how she could not show her children any ounce of affection. We did have some moments of comfort growing up, thanks to Gram. At least she read to us, held us, and showed us that we mattered.

As an adult, it became more and more uncomfortable to be around my mother. This was not the same for some of my siblings.

They continued to have relationships with her all through their adulthood. As for me, I just couldn't. I needed to separate myself from the past in order to attain my greatest achievement: a happy, loving, caring family. Our relationship never connected. I feel like she saw her children not as an extension of herself but more as the offspring of the men who broke her heart, abused her, or left town. But knowing what I know now, was our relationship doomed from the start because I was the consequence of her "dirty little secret" that haunted her? Every time she looked at me, did she see him? Or maybe we were a great deal alike: stubborn and vindictive, so that subconsciously, we were both waiting for the other to make the first call. At this point, do I really think she would have wanted to apologize for all this time and attempted to reconnect? If I had reached out to her and tried to mend what was so far broken, would she have at some point confessed her secret? Maybe after my father or Gram had passed away, she could no longer have gotten in trouble with them. Would this have meant I could have met Chef Louis before he passed?

All these questions swirled through my mind, becoming a whispered plea for a reality that had slipped away now that she was gone. If I was partially to blame for our relationship, could I have included her in my life and, more importantly, my family's life? My father remarried after Marge passed away, so my children did have a grandmother figure in their life.

After all that my mother had put us through, I didn't want to rekindle any relationship with her. The hypocrisy of it all was more than I could handle. It was more than just moving on from the past. It was trying to live the rest of my life after lacking any emotional love and support from a parent during my upbringing, my most impressionable years.

There were a few moments within the last forty years where she and I were in the same place at the same time: mostly family barbecues at my sisters' houses or my niece's wedding held at, you guessed it, the club. I knew she was invited and would be a guest that day. Of course she was; she was my niece's grandmother. I remember it was one of the hottest days in July, and I can still feel the beads of sweat that gathered on my forehead to this day. There was something about seeing her at my workplace, sitting at a cocktail table with my aunt, that was paralyzing. I believe my daughter introduced herself to her grandmother for the first time that night. Me? I steered clear.

Duke

After my mother's death I was the lowest I'd been in years. I'd dealt with periods of depression my whole life, but this was different, and I wasn't sure I could shake it off or compartmentalize my feelings as I always had done. Unable to sleep, my mind would be racing from one parent to the other, reliving everything I could remember them doing or saying. Examining each one and all their flaws. Every memory, every story, every shortcoming. I couldn't help but wonder if any of them ever really loved me? Feeling unwanted and unloved by my parents has left me with a hunger worse than our time receiving cheese and bread from the government.

"Well, I'm heading into work now," Kim said, as I stared at the bedroom wall, fully wrapped in our comforter. "I'm sure Sadie would love to go for a walk later," she hinted as she left the bedroom. I had told her I was taking the day off or would come in later. I listened as she went down the stairs and out the garage door. Sadie picked her head up to watch Kim leave, yet she didn't move from my side. Dogs can sense things. And as much as she probably agreed with Kim about going for that walk later, she knew her loyalty meant lying in bed with me a little longer. Truthfully, I don't think she minded.

From across the room, I heard my iPad ring. I had ignored calls or texts over the last few days, but this chime was different. I knew this sound. Facebook Messenger had a different tone, so I knew it was him replying to a message I had sent him the day before. I was still reeling from my mother dying and any chance of getting answers out of her. Despite not wanting to leave the comfort of my bed, I knew he somehow would make me feel better. I had to see him.

"Hey, Duke. Are you free today? Would love to see you," I quietly said.

"Why yes, brother," he replied. "It would be lovely to see you today." We agreed to meet at the diner where we'd had lunch before, just about halfway between our homes. Since it was already afternoon, we decided to make it an early dinner.

"Perfect! See you there, Brother!" I said, with the slightest bit of joy creeping into my voice.

We hadn't gotten together in a few weeks, and I craved his comforting smile. I also had been avoiding telling him that my mother passed away. I didn't want him to be disappointed that she left, taking her secrets to the grave.

I rolled into the Queen Diner in Glenville well before the dinner rush. Once again, Duke was waiting in the parking lot for me.

"Brother," he said as he went in for a hug. He held me tight, and it felt like my whole body melted into his arms at that moment.

"How are you doing?" he kindly asked, despite already knowing my answer. He had such a tender way about him. He knew I was in a dark place, and he held onto me tightly. I always felt so secure in his presence.

"Not so good. I have some news," I said, my voice beginning to shake. We went inside and were directed to an open booth. Soon after we got situated, a waitress came with menus and poured us coffee.

"Remember how my sisters were going to take our father's picture to my mother...to see if she remembered anything?" I asked Duke right away. There was no sense in waiting before I shared this news with him. He nodded.

"Well, they did. She saw the picture. She saw the picture of our father but never answered any of my questions. She..." I paused as I took another breath. "She actually passed away."

"I'm sorry, she what?" Duke asked, never breaking eye contact with me.

"Yeah, it turns out she saw the picture and died a few hours later. Isn't that something?" I awkwardly chuckled as I broke the news.

I picked up my coffee cup and took a sip as Duke stared at me, jaw gaping. Just then, the waitress returned to see if we were ready to order lunch, but something told me that she caught on to the uncomfortable moment and, without asking, decided to give us a few more minutes.

Duke grabbed a hold of my hands from across the table. "Oh, Brother, I am so very sorry to hear this. God bless her and your family."

"It's just so wild, you know? Why then?" I let go of Duke's hands. "Why did she have to die right then? I haven't needed her for ANYTHING in fifty years, but now, the one time I needed her to share some information about my life, she goes and dies? Giving me no chance to learn more about our father and their relationship. But of course, she let me down my whole life; why wouldn't she let me down again?"

My mouth was like a volcano. Everything that had been building up for the last few weeks came gushing out—burning lava spewing everywhere. Duke reached out to grab my hands again. Like one of those weighted blankets, his touch calmed me down and eased my anxiety.

"Take a breath," he said as he held onto me. He took a deep breath, too. "Well, she saw his picture, right? I am sure she recognized him. And frankly, I don't see this as her letting you down. Maybe she chose never to tell anyone as a way of protecting you. Who knows what your life would have been like if she had confessed all of this when you were young."

"If she had only come clean after I had children or after my father died, I might have had the opportunity to meet him," I stammered. "I think she at least owed me that. But how do I just move on from this? I'll never be able to forgive her or Louis, or any of them for that matter. They all failed us. They failed us as parents," I said, nervously playing with the paper seal that held our napkin roll-up. My emotions were spiraling. These events all happened so fast: DNA results, finding Duke, learning about Chef Louis and our professional resemblance, trying to question my mother after all this time, and her dying. It was all becoming too much to process.

"Listen," Duke said as he reached back for my hands. "My father made many mistakes, as did your parents. None of them would have won any 'parent of the year' awards," he said as he chuckled softly. "We all know my father was a womanizer, an absent father, and treated our mother, his children, and grandchildren poorly." Duke admitted that he was still harboring some resentment not only for himself but for how his father had treated his mother and siblings throughout the years. I could sense he was treading on very personal and emotional topics. I started to feel bad that I raised this whole issue and was insensitive to his emotions.

He continued, "They may have all been poor parents, but they made us who we are. You have lived your life based on their choices, and you have your beautiful life to show for it. I have learned in my years that forgiveness is a funny thing. It cannot change the past. It does not dismiss the choices that any of them made. But it's about you now. Forgiving your parents can only help you heal and move on."

Duke was right. I may be disappointed with each one of my parents; however, I worked my ass off to live my life without making those same parenting mistakes. They taught me and all my siblings what *not* to be as a parent, and in turn, we could all raise happy and healthy families.

"What you have to remember is what a wonderful family you have. You spent years of your life living through the effects of trauma, and you had the guts to say, 'this ends with me' and did everything so your children felt loved and cared for."

We finished up our lunch, and as we hugged goodbye, I thanked him for listening to my babbling about the past. I felt like I just left the confessional and was given no penance. Duke always had a way of grounding me and bringing me back to what was really important: family. I'm so lucky to have him as a brother and friend. I couldn't help but think about what he said about forgiving them. There were so many times in my life in which I made excuses for each of my parents: that's just the way it was back then...they all had childhood issues of their own...they dealt with so many pressures on their own but they lacked any substantial resources...they all did what they thought was best at the time. Other times, I would blame the booze. I had witnessed so many lives destroyed or families ripped apart because of alcohol abuse, it just seemed like a common situation, so they all got a pass in my mind. However, just because I accepted them for who they were, never meant that I ever could forgive any of them. Still, I couldn't get past what Duke said to me. Forgiveness isn't something you do for anyone else, it's a part of your own recovery. In order for me to heal and move forward, I needed to be able to see all my parents for who they were, to forgive but never forget. And in retrospect, this process might have been more painful than the original wounds I had suffered.

Forgiveness

My mother didn't have it easy. She was a spoiled, adopted child of a strict older couple. They tried to set boundaries, but that only intensified her behaviors. Perhaps she was the way she was because she craved the love of her own mother, who didn't want her and was unfit to care for her. (Ironic, don't you think?) There is no doubt in anyone's mind that my mother had severe mental illness with a mix of postpartum depression. Unfortunately, that can be genetic. To fill her void, she clenched on to any man who would provide her an ounce of attention.

As she kept having children, the only solution to "make things better" back then was a hysterectomy. But even after her surgery and hospital stay in 1962, why did things get even worse? There was no Xanax, Prozac, or Trintellix in those days. Her behavior was so erratic that there was no way that she could have handled the depression without medical treatments, on top of managing the needs of the household and her seven children. I can't imagine how many diapers my mother had to wash. She went years with at least three children in diapers. They had no money then, so they couldn't afford the company that would pick up dirty diapers, wash them, and return them clean and folded. So, she had to handwash piles of diapers on top of our regular clothes plus an intense number of bedsheets, as one of us always wet the bed, probably long past what would be considered appropriate for an average child. Add the stress of trying to keep us all fed. Yes, most of our meals came from the government, but that did require her to file for welfare, which was an effort.

She did what she could, especially through all the domestic tension and abuse, even more so after my father left. I could only imagine the pressure she felt to continue when she was alone with all seven of us. So, did that give her a pass for all the verbal and physical abuse and neglect? That was a tough one. She was so erratic that the slightest situation resulted in us being beaten. It was obvious now that she was projecting her own trauma and insecurities, unconsciously externalizing her inner demons and forcing them on us. She had no choice. However, as a father, I had no clue how she could have deliberately hurt her children, time after time. Could I forgive my mother for her infidelity? Of course, I thought. If she hadn't, I would not be here. Maybe not even my younger siblings. It wasn't the classiest move, with two young children from a previous marriage, two years after Laurie was born, recently married to my father. But, knowing what I knew now, she probably was not getting what she needed from my father, so she had no choice but to be seduced by the next man who showed her an ounce of attention—pushed to a brief one-night stand due to my father's carousing, drinking, and instability. Did her infidelity exacerbate my father's behavior? Or vice versa? It was hard to blame her for that. Could I forgive her for dying and not confessing to my discovery? As angry as I was that she never had to admit to her infidelity, it truly made me think about what I needed from her anyway. Would I have felt different if she looked at the picture and said, "Yep! That's your dad."? There was no uncertainty regarding the DNA results and my relationship with Duke and Ricky. And I had ruled out the possibility that the father who raised me knew, since he never showed any indication or treated me any other way than as his son. I really didn't need her confession after all.

Truthfully, my father was most likely just as responsible for my mother's erratic behavior. He wasn't the best provider, especially when he and my mother were together. His binge drinking and instigating didn't help matters whatsoever. I was sure most of this was due to him being abandoned by his father at the age of ten, which cast a deep sense of bitter resentment that he never could overcome. Yet, forgiving my father seemed to be easier for me. He did attempt to keep the dysfunctional family together, and supported my mother when she was ill and in the hospital. Even through their intense marital issues, I knew that they really did care for each other. My father also did everything he could to find us and keep us together when my mother sent us off to the children's home. If he didn't fight for us as a family, then we could have all been adopted into different families or, worse, sent to St. Colman's. When the state could not find homes for older children, they were often sent to St. Colman's, the Catholic school and home for unwanted children. In the 1990s, the school made national news for decades of child abuse and molestation. When it closed, records were released that showed hundreds of complaints of sexual abuse buried by the church. This, in my mind, couldn't be minimized. So, in my mind, my father redeemed himself for his part in our tumultuous childhood.

Furthermore, once he rescued us from the shelter, he didn't hesitate to bring his five kids in with his new wife and her six kids. Marge never wanted to raise eleven children, but she did because she loved him, and that's what they had to do. Once we moved into the Junction, our lives were stabilized. It was not rainbows and butterflies by any means, with knockdown, dragged-out arguments over the stereotypical stepchildren, and wicked stepmother syndrome. Understandably, my father often sided with Marge, as he felt guilty for bringing five more children into her life. They had to stretch their dollars, food, and clothing now that they had blended their families. Marge had to cook for twice as many kids and manage the already relatively sparse family budget, resulting in my father working two and three part-time jobs to make ends meet. Luckily, she was a great cook. By the time I lived with them, I knew that there was no Santa, and all those Christmas gifts for all eleven of us were purchased by them, which probably set them back quite a bit each year. And I always thought my half siblings' presents were not what they could have been without having us five to buy for. I'm assuming that is why receiving gifts at Christmas is still very uncomfortable for me.

As I remember, Marge's anger was mainly projected verbally with the occasional spanking. I was a little more tolerant than my siblings because at thirteen, I could empathize and understand Marge's position. Sure, she came down on me for things, forcing me to do more chores than the others. I remember I always had to shovel the horse manure from the garage stall where Jo-Anne kept her prize-possession horse she bought with her father's insurance policy. I would grumble as I scooped, but I didn't mind because I liked Jo-Anne and looked up to her. Unlike some of my siblings, I never felt a need to be angry with Marge. We were the intruders, and for the most part, our half siblings accepted us being there. Maybe we all saw it differently, or I overlooked Marge's toughness because I felt fortunate to be together and no longer facing the unknown.

As I attempted to find forgiveness for each of my parents, I couldn't help but include Chef Louis. Was his womanizing and scoundrel behavior forgivable? Adding my mother and Ricky's mother (and possibly many more women) to the notches in his belt? I wasn't sure about forgiveness, but I understood the behavior and maybe a little of what he had to deal with trying to be a successful chef and entrepreneur. His focus was to achieve greatness in his career, which sometimes meant moving around the country to find better jobs. He did what was necessary to support his family financially and achieve his career goals. Louis could have just abandoned his family, but he continued to be an absent father, sending money home and eventually paying off the mortgage. And the foundation of the restaurant business is made up of constant inappropriate sexual innuendos and intense flirtatious interactions, mixed with a significant number of drugs, alcohol, and pretty low morals. It is common for the front of house staff to "hook up" with someone from the kitchen staff. It was no surprise that Chef Louis was able to make eyes at my mother and sweep her off her feet. I couldn't blame him for any of that. Now, I assumed he could have kept his restaurant open if I hadn't come along. But his professional drive would have never settled until he worked at the big hotels and country clubs out west, making a name for himself and achieving fame and recognition in the culinary world. Did I resent him for never reaching out to me at any point? No, because I believed he knew that if he did, it would only cause more harm than good to my family.

Not Step, Not Half, Just Family

Driving home from my early bird dinner with Duke, I came up with an idea. Talking with Duke helped me see there was no sense in living in a dark cave of resentment. I needed to forgive those who were no longer with us and appreciate those still in my life. This was for no other reason than for me to heal and accept my life for what it was. I forgave my parents not because they deserved it, but because I deserved to move on. For so long, I had avoided my family, especially my half siblings, for no other reason than I was running and hiding from my past. Talking with Duke made me realize that life is short, so I went full force into planning mode.

Duke, Ricky, and I had spoken about meeting together at some point soon. Duke and I were lucky enough to live in the same area, so we met in person, but we knew we needed an opportunity to see Ricky, not just through an iPad. We had spoken about getting together in person this summer, and I was so excited on my drive that I called Kim to brainstorm.

"What if we do it at the end of August?" I asked Kim on speakerphone.

"Sure," she replied cautiously. It was quite unlike me to be the one instigating family gatherings. She had always been the representative for our family to accept or decline invitations for family events. For me to be excited to plan something? She stayed leery. "Are you sure you want to get together with Duke, Ricky, and their families? That's a lot of people you don't really know. I can't see you feeling comfortable talking to all of them for very long," she said matter-of-factly. Hell, she wasn't wrong, and this definitely was something out of my comfort zone, but I was starting to get annoyed with her being such a buzzkill.

"We have been discussing meeting in person since we first met on Zoom. They are my brothers! I want to get to know them and their lives. And figure out more of my life!"

At this point, Kim had no words. Obviously, she remained supportive, but my excitement for this was extremely foreign to her.

"We can figure this out more when I get home. I'll be there in a few," I said as I hit the Bluetooth button on my steering wheel to end the call. As I made my way home, the potential ideas swirled in my head, and my plan snowballed. I pulled into the driveway and was greeted by Sadie, slowly creeping out of the garage door. I had left earlier in such a dark mood it was as if she had spent the entire time I was gone worrying about me.

"Hi, Sadie! Who's Daddy's girl? Who's my good girl?" I said as I smothered her with pets and scratches. I'm sure she could tell, based on my raised pitch, that my mood improved while I was gone. I beelined directly to my office to set up a Zoom meeting with Duke and Ricky. As I waited for them to sign on, I lit a new cigar and took a long drag.

"End of August works for us!" Ricky said enthusiastically after I had presented my plan to them.

"You know I am in!" chimed Duke and gave me a wink. He knew he must have gotten through to me at dinner and was proud of my initiative.

The three of us were "over the moon" excited. This would be the first time the three of us would be together in person. It felt a bit surreal. It was one thing by Zoom, but now, in person? It would be a gesture of tribute to the incredible journey we were going through together. Over the next few days, the three of us sent ideas of things to do the weekend Ricky came into town. Ricky suggested having dinner at a local staple for great seafood. He made the reservation for Friday night at the Reel Seafood Co. Duke and his son-in-law, Dave, wanted to make sure the three of us made our way to the Saratoga Race Course. Duke and Dave went regularly, and it seemed to be a classic "must-do" activity for those visiting in the summer. We scheduled that for Saturday. That left me Sunday. I offered my house to have a barbecue. I told them we could grill and that they and their wives should bring bathing suits. What I didn't tell them was my bigger idea...I still needed more time to think about how I would pull it all off. All I knew was that the end of August couldn't come soon enough.

Kim and I began planning the barbecue for that Sunday.

"We could get some of the food from the club to grill," Kim suggested. "How many people do we think?" As she began to count our family, Duke and his family, and Ricky and his wife, I stopped her.

"What if we invite everyone? All of my siblings."

Kim raised her head and stared at me dumbfounded. The effort she usually had to go through to convince me to attend my family's Christmas party or, worse, when it was our turn to host the Christmas party, was strenuous enough. Now, I was trying to plan a summer picnic with my entire family. She continued to stare at me. I could tell she was struggling to process what I was doing.

"Everyone," I continued. "Every half, step, whole sibling. Let's get everyone here!" My excitement was beginning to alarm her at this point. Any other time, this idea would be my nightmare. This meant every one of my siblings, stepbrothers and sisters, half brothers and sisters, and all their families. Some had never met, and many hadn't seen each other in twenty, thirty, or forty years. But this time was different. This time, I wanted all my siblings to be there. This time, I needed them to be. This family gathering would be the perfect way for everyone to meet and be together. And I know not our mother, father, Marge, nor Chef Louis sure as hell would have ever imagined this day happening!

As we planned, I got more excited for this moment. Throughout this journey, I had done everything possible to ensure my siblings never felt like I was trading or taking on a new family while leaving my old one behind. I wanted this gathering to be where all my siblings could meet, talk, share stories, and make new memories, regardless of who their parents were. So, the planning commenced! Courtney whipped up a great festive flier in her usual teacher mode to share with every family. We mailed paper fliers to some and sent the digital copy all over Facebook. We made sure everyone from our family was included. Word got out, and we waited for responses. The timing was perfect because my stepsister Jo-Anne typically lives in Florida but would be at their property near Howes Caverns, only about forty minutes away. I also contacted my brother Jeff in Ocean City, Maryland. Summer could be tricky, and I was hopeful he and his family could make it work.

As I checked for RSVPs on Facebook, I saw a post from my stepsister, Donna. It was an image that said, "Not half, Not full, Just family." It was then I realized that there was no bigger truth for me in my life now than that statement. We were forever connected and intertwined profoundly during our formative years, shaping us into who we were. This barbecue would be a pivotal moment in which all siblings would come together, regardless of who their parents were or any mixed feelings and tangled memories that may still live on.

A few weeks before the party, Kim and I sat at our kitchen island discussing the final details when she asked me a simple question.

"Are you sure you want to do this?"

The question hit me as if something was punching me from the inside. She wasn't being negative, she was just concerned. This was so out of character for me. She loved and knew me so well, she just wanted to ensure I wanted this before I followed through. She reminded me how the last time we had just some of my family at our house, I had hinted at using police tape to barricade myself in the kitchen and kick everyone else out.

"I'm just worried about how you will feel after everything that happened this year. I don't want anything to get tense or uncomfortable for you or anyone."

She was right. What if this whole thing was a mistake? After all, there was a lot of history, and who knew how everyone was taking my news. Would they be upset that I "opened Pandora's box" to begin with? The last thing I wanted was for any of my siblings to think I would abandon them or love them less because of this new life discovery.

Furthermore, some of us hadn't seen each other in years, so why would they come now? Just because I was trying to reconnect did not necessarily mean they wanted to. Why was I forcing this on everyone? It's not like I liked the attention. Old familiar feelings of anxiety and panic filled my body. I recently read Matthew Perry's memoir, and he wrote words that resonated with me at this moment. "I'm not enough, I don't matter, I'm too needy. These thoughts make me uncomfortable. I need love, but I don't trust it. If I dropped my character and showed you who I really am, you might notice me. Or worse, you might notice me and leave me."

I left the kitchen island and entered the dark living room. I lay on my couch, covered myself with my blanket, and shut my eyes. Sadie, of course, followed me and took her position on the floor beside me. She was reluctant but knew her job. It was three p.m. on a Sunday afternoon, but I was done for the day.

Even though invitations had gone out, I was ready to pull the plug on the entire party. We would figure out how to still get together with Duke and Ricky during the weekend, but I could not have everyone at my house for this reunion. I lay on my couch for the rest of the night. What was I thinking? I loved my family, but why on earth would I plan for all of them to come to this? Just for me? Just because my life was turned upside down didn't mean it had to be their life, too. None of my other siblings found out they had a different father, so why would they want to meet Duke and Ricky?

Just then, the phone rang from my desk in the office. I didn't move. I didn't want to talk to anyone. I let the call go to voicemail as I rolled over to face the back of the couch.

"Ping." My cell text tone went off, presumably from the person who had just called.

"Ping...ping...ping." Three more texts behind it. Alright, whoever this was had a lot to say to me. I slowly tossed the blanket off, stood up, and shuffled into the office. I picked my phone up to see the four texts from my brother, Jeff, from Maryland. He hadn't yet confirmed whether he would be able to come up for the barbecue.

Hey, brother!

I can't wait to see you soon.

And the family!

And meet your new brothers!

I read those texts over and over again. This was all I needed to hear. My little brother, whom I had cherished since the day he was born, was excited to see me and meet my new half brothers. I knew this was the right decision and I had to go through with this party.

The weekend finally arrived. All my anticipation and excitement overcame any ounce of anxiety that I may have felt. Ricky had made the reservation for dinner at the Reel Seafood restaurant for Friday night. We decided to meet there, as we all came from different directions. I still remember how I felt, seeing Ricky walking in the parking lot. We hugged instantly, like we had known each other for years. There was something so surreal about meeting someone I knew was my half brother, but I was just meeting for the first time as an adult. Duke and Edna then arrived, and our crew began sharing introductions, pleasantries, and, of course, hugs. Once inside, we were seated at a lovely banquette along the window. Kim and I hoped to run into the owner, LeGrande Serras, one of the region's most successful restaurateurs. The Real Seafood restaurant was a longtime favorite for decades. It remained stuck in the eighties, with a vintage flair and the same menu with little change over the years, but if it's not broken, why fix it? I first met LeGrande when he was a young man, running Peggy's Restaurant in downtown Schenectady. He and his family would have Sunday dinner at the Turf Tavern restaurant, where I worked early on. The owners, Steve and Fanny Karamanos, were close to the LeGrande family and would have an early dinner after church. In fact, just weeks before, Kim spoke to LeGrande and told him of my story and that my biological father had a restaurant. LeGrande clearly remembered the restaurant in the fifties opened by Chef Lou Caruso.

That evening, we had a wonderful dinner filled with sharing stories and memories. We each took turns talking about our lives and making connections with each other. All night felt like a perfect mix of surrealism and comfort. It was beyond special to be sitting with these brothers after all this time. Before we left for the night, Kim made sure to document the evening with the first of many brother photos.

Saturday was a beautiful day. We made our way up to the Saratoga Race Course. Dave had arranged our tickets, so he met us at the gate since he had to work. The warm summer sun beat down, but we had seats close to the upper mezzanine so we could get out of the sun periodically, especially when we went to place our bets. It was a wonderful day, and although none of us had much luck with the ponies, we all just enjoyed each other's company like we had known each other for years. I have always felt like my participation in group settings can be awkward and uncomfortable. I assume it is because I never feel like the other person wants to hear what I say. But it was different with them. There was no uneasiness or tension when we were together; it just felt comfortable, which was something I was unfamiliar with. Those two days were a perfect start to a fantastic weekend, and we all were looking forward to our sibling reunion on Sunday. Before the weekend, I had heard from my other siblings about how excited they were to reconnect and meet Duke and Ricky. I was almost becoming overwhelmed with joy as we prepared for the day.

Like when we hosted the Christmas party at my house, I planned on cooking, serving, and cleaning up the mess afterward.

"Are you crazy?" Kim said. "This is your party and your family...you are the host! You are not working!"

So, Kim arranged for chafing dishes to warm the food, tables, and chairs to be delivered from the club—one of the few perks of being the manager there. We also asked Elaine, one of our favorite servers, to help care for everything. We had known her since my time at The Edison Club, and she was just as much part of our family, so I knew she would be the perfect fit. Just knowing she would be there to handle the food, drinks, and dishes so I could mingle was a massive weight off my shoulders. And for the first time at a family party, I didn't feel the need to get out the police tape.

One by one, family members entered the backyard: my sisters Debbie, Rae Ann, Laurie, and Toni and their families, my little brother Jeff and his wife Cindy, my stepsiblings Donna, Jake, and Jo-Anne and their families, and my new half brothers Duke, Ricky, and their families. My mother's younger sister, Donna, was there too, as she was an essential family member and would never miss a get-together. The atmosphere was filled with joy and laughter as everyone gathered. I can still remember looking over my deck well into the evening to see Jake and Jeff, who hadn't seen each other since they were about six, chatting away as if the last half-century never happened. My oldest sister, Toni, had never met Marge's kids, as she had left home and was not around when we moved in with my father. What I found most interesting was in the many conversations that day, no one brought up our parents. No one cared about who each other's mother or father was. We were siblings who had all been through a lot, but we knew we were fortunate enough to be a part of this family.

We couldn't have asked for better weather that whole weekend. It was the most beautiful summer day. The kids could swim and play in the inflatable bounce house that I had set up for them, and everyone was comfortable enough to sit outside without fighting for shade. After a few hours of eating and mingling, Courtney said, "Let's get some pictures!" and directed everyone to gather on one side of the pool. "Taller ones in the back!" she barked, as if all her third graders were heading out to recess. "Let's have the little kids sit on the edge of the pool in front," she said, keeping everyone organized. There we were, all smiles and together as one loving extended family. As we took photos, I realized this might have been the first time I genuinely enjoyed myself around my family. I was proud of us and proud to be a part of this family. No matter our genetics, we were a family. Not step, not half, just family. We created memories woven together by our bond that would endure long after this barbecue.

Just around dusk, groups started to say their goodbyes. We all hugged and promised to get together sooner rather than later. As Elaine cleaned up the last few tables, she approached me and gave me the most genuine hug.

"You have a wonderful family," she whispered.

"I sure do," I replied, grinning ear to ear.

As the final puzzle piece clicked into place, a deep sense of satisfaction washed over me, a perfect moment of contentment as maybe I helped all of us heal a little more that day. After all, what was more important than family?

Epilogue

Five years have passed since I stumbled upon those keys and opened the "hidden boxes in the attic." As someone who spent all my life working towards the next big project, I never could have imagined that my next big project would be writing my memoir. When I finally got to a point where I felt comfortable enough to retire, I assumed my days would be spent relaxing, putzing around the house on my "Honey Do List," and working in my garden. I never thought the first few years of my retirement would be spent reliving a life I spent so many years avoiding. Author Anaïs Nin once said, "We write to taste life twice, in the moment and in retrospect."

This process has given me the keys that have unlocked the chains of the past. As much as my perspective on things has changed over the last few years, one thing for sure hasn't changed: none of this was my or my siblings' fault. My biological inheritance does not change my love for them by any means. In fact, it has brought me closer to all of them than ever before, and I now feel a greater responsibility to be there for them in any way I can. We all have struggled through our lives and have learned to cope with the physical and emotional scars from our childhood. We have each lived a life haunted by our past, yet we are resilient and determined to move forward. I am immensely proud of how each of us broke the generational dysfunction and raised wonderful, well-loved families.

Since our family reunion, Duke, Ricky, and I have maintained a close relationship, and we are each thankful to have the others and their families in our lives. I would be remiss if I didn't acknowledge how lucky I was to find such wonderful, accepting people. It is said that each NPE (Not Parent Expected) affects upwards of fifty additional family members, friends, and colleagues. Everyone has a similar story or knows someone who found relatives they did not know existed through genetic testing. Unfortunately, many DNA surprises tear families apart when these secrets come to light. The newfound relatives are only sometimes receptive to the news, and often flat-out reject any attempt at a conversation.

I am blessed and couldn't have asked for a better outcome. Ricky has traveled to the Albany area several times, including making a special trip with Cindy to attend my son's wedding, joining Duke and Kim at our table.

Duke and I have been able to get together numerous times for coffee, lunch, or family dinners at our favorite Italian restaurants. The excitement and novelty of the situation may have worn off, but we are as close as any half brothers thrust together this late in life could be. In the last few years, the world has also been hit with a global pandemic, limiting our social interactions and hindering us from seeing each other as often as we would like. Yet, through the magic of technology, we could still connect through Zoom video calls as much as possible. Sadly, during this time, we also said goodbye to Duke's beloved wife, Edna, and our youngest half brother, Jake.

After receiving my DNA results on that Valentine's Day many years ago, my life has been forever changed. I expanded my family circle. I discovered the truth about where I came from and half my DNA. I connected and accepted Chef Louis through shared memories and stories. I questioned, struggled, challenged, and fought with whether or not my mother knew who my real father was.

Although this secret was ultimately exposed, I'd be lying if I said I wasn't left with more questions and "what-ifs" to ponder for the rest of my days.

Nevertheless, this experience has taught me that acceptance is a form of forgiveness and is not mutually exclusive. I accepted all my parents for who they were. I am finally able to see that forgiving them was the closure I always needed, and I harbor no more resentment. I can now embrace my life, and my family, as it is.

Acknowledgements

To my daughter and co-author Courtney who I had the great pleasure of working closely with on this project: I appreciate your time, guidance, editing skills, and willingness to spend hundreds of hours over the last four years making this book possible. I'm very proud of you and hope you enjoyed the ride as much as I have.

To Rachael Herron, author, teacher, and composition coach: Thank you for sharing your immense wealth of literary knowledge, allowing me to be in your master classes and supporting me throughout this entire process. I would not have been able to finish this book without your belief and encouragement every step of the way. I will be forever grateful.

Thanks to Catriona Turner for your timely editing, attention to detail, and professional input. We couldn't have done this without your support.

To my writing community and fellow writers, Aylene, Heather, Jason, Lisa, Susan, Michele, Nirmy, Rosie, and the rest of the BAMFS. Your friendship and encouragement pushed me to continue writing week in and week out to see this project to its conclusion. BAMFS for life!

Made in United States
North Haven, CT
15 March 2024

50046846R00141